Kabbalistic Contemplations

Kabbalistic Contemplations

Z'ev ben Shimon Halevi

Kabbalah Society

Bet El Trust
Registered Charity No. 288712

This edition published by:

www.kabbalahsociety.org
E-mail: books@kabbalahsociety.org

A CIP catalogue record for this book is available from the British Library.

ISBN 978-1-909171-47-3

Design by Tree of Life Publishing
www.treeoflifepublishing.co.uk

To

Isaac ben Abraham of Posquières

Master Teacher

By the same author:

Adam and the Kabbalistic Trees
A Kabbalistic Universe
The Way of Kabbalah
Introduction to the World of Kabbalah
The Kabbalist at Work
Kabbalah and Exodus
Kabbalah: School of the Soul
Psychology and Kabbalah
The Kabbalistic Tree of Life
Kabbalah and Astrology
The Anointed—*A Kabbalistic Novel*
The Anatomy of Fate
The Path of a Kabbalist
A Kabbalistic View of History

By other publishers:

Kabbalah—The Divine Plan (HarperCollins)
Kabbalah: Tradition of Hidden Knowledge (Thames & Hudson)
Astrology: The Celestial Mirror (Thames & Hudson)
As Above, So Below (Stuart & Watkins)

Contents

List of Illustrations

Figure 1—KABBALIST
The seeker after Truth wears a protective garment of discipline and carries the staff of knowledge, both of which are essential for navigating the higher Worlds. Without this equipment, one would be overwhelmed by the sheer power and scale of the macrocosm and invisible dimensions beyond the sphere of the mundane. (Engraving, 16th century)

Foreword

This book started as an idea to focus on the Way of Contemplation. Each short chapter together with an image or a diagram is meant to be a starting point for further thought, contemplation or discussion as well as to provide material for study groups.

Unfortunately my late husband did not have time to finish this book which is now published posthumously. As we worked together on a previous draft, it became my task to bring the book to a conclusion. It is the result of numerous conversations and script conferences as well as participating in study groups where these topics were discussed. It has been a great privilege to be part of this Work.

Rebekah Kenton
London, Spring 2021

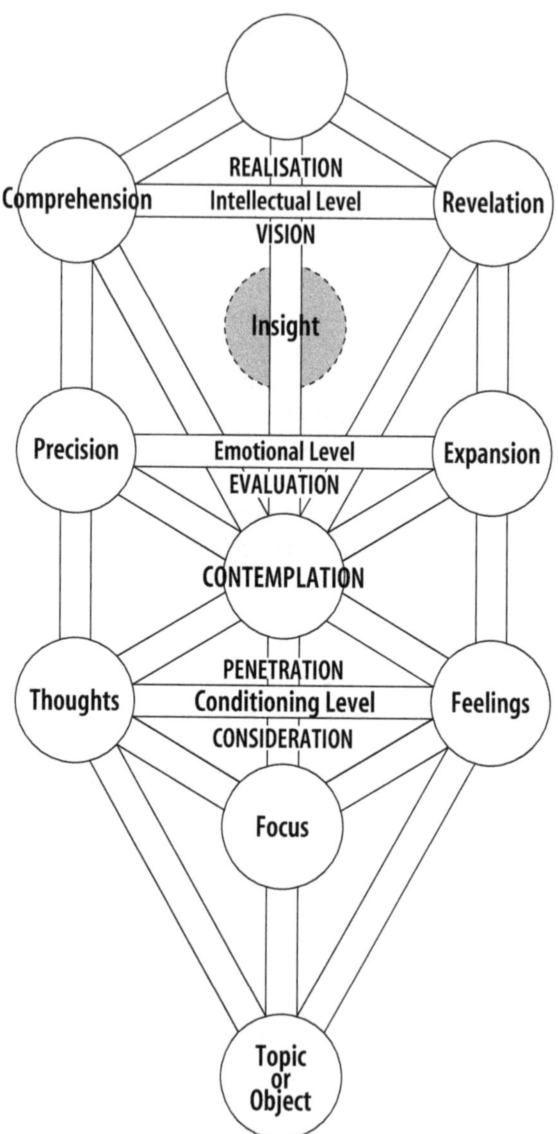

Figure 2—TREE OF CONTEMPLATION

The Way of Contemplation complements the Ways of Action and Devotion. In esoteric work, we need to practise all three modes in order to increase our capability. However, we should be aware that some psychological processes can help or hinder the levels of conscious contemplation. (Halevi)

Introduction

That which is written down may be authentic but this does not guarantee its veracity. Ancient texts, however academically respectable, can range from the facile to the profound. The hallmark of a penetrating understanding is a simplicity that goes to the essence of a topic. Cross-references about where, when and who wrote a text can obscure the actual meaning of what was said.

The Book of Exodus is not just an historical account but an allegory of the inner journey from psychological slavery, through the desert of the soul's purification, to the Promised Land of the Spirit. The Bible began as an oral line and its form is a mixture of fact and mythology. Later, the esoteric or hidden metaphysics of the Bible stories were seen as recognisable stages of cosmic and human development. This phase belonged to the Middle Ages.

Today we have the added tools of science and modern psychology which give us a more precise understanding of the reality behind the everyday world. The pictures, words and diagrams in this book present an overall view that can be seen to govern the most mundane as well as the higher levels of Existence. The art of contemplation is to penetrate each topic and relate it to the principles of the Tree of Life and Jacob's Ladder. During a profound contemplation, a shift in perception of Existence may occur.

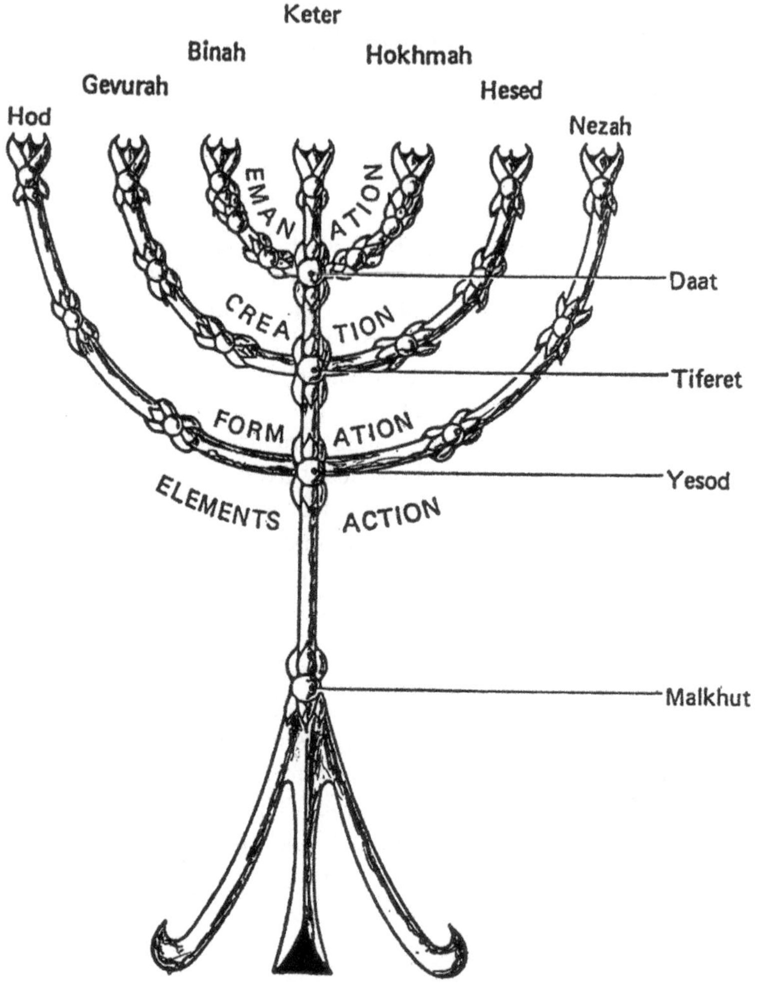

Figure 3—MENORAH

The language of the Bible is symbolism. To the discerning mind the metaphysics behind the biblical myths, history and characters are revealed in their archetypal essence. The Menorah is not just a sacred symbol of light but a metaphysical image of the Divine Realm and its dynamic order. (Drawing by Halevi)

Consideration

The Menorah contains the esoteric symbolism and kabbalistic principles embedded in the Bible. On the summit of the holy mountain of Sinai where Heaven and Earth meet, God gave the design to Moses. This sacred object was to be made out of a single piece of gold, symbolising the essential unity of the Divine realm. It was to have a vertical axis in the centre and two side wings. These three fundamental principles are found in every esoteric tradition. They represent the active and passive processes while the central pivot of equilibrium, or the Will of the Holy One, governs the balance of Existence.

One may also observe that there are four levels within the design. They correspond to the four Worlds in Kabbalah while the nodal points set out the sefirot, the primordial principles that govern each World. They are complemented by twenty-two decorations which represent the paths between the sefirot as well as the Hebrew alphabet. Altogether they compose the twelve triads of the metaphysical system known in Kabbalah as the Tree of Life.

All these factors can be discerned in the process of contemplation in which layer upon layer of information is analysed and synthesised. Once this archetypal system is recognised, then intuition begins to perceive these principles at work not only in the higher Worlds but also in everyday life. The emotional response may be that of wonder.

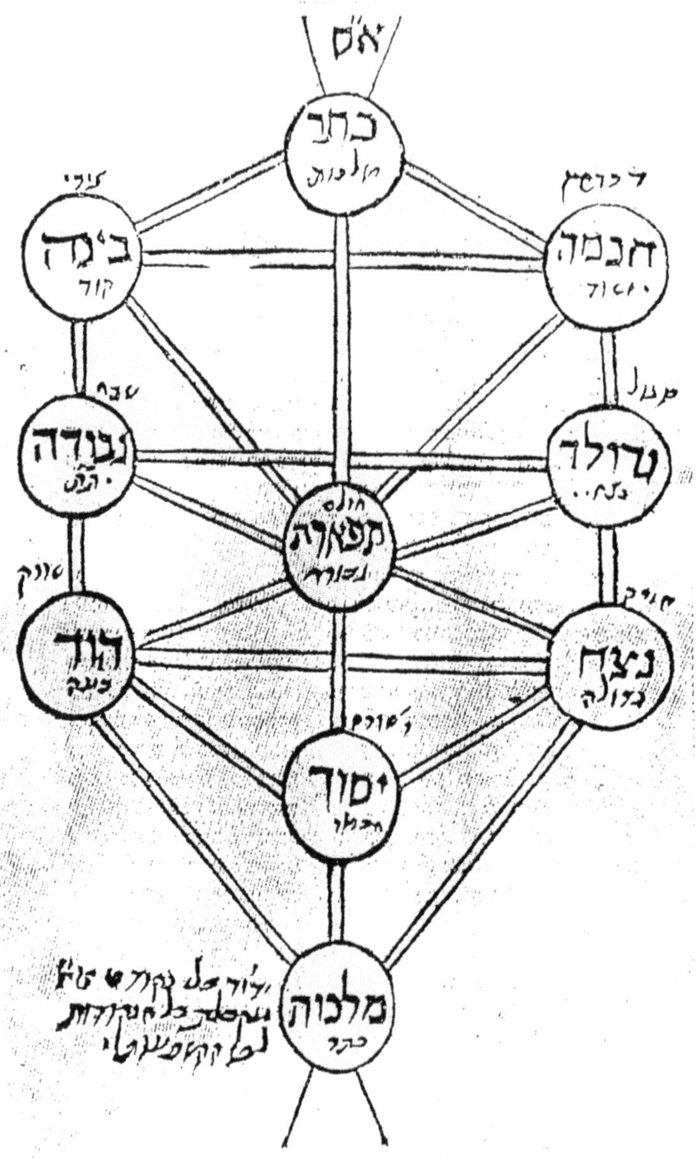

Figure 4—BASICS
The Tree is the chief tool of the Kabbalist. With understanding its principles, structure and dynamic, many things can become clear. Once the Tree is integrated into the mind and the heart, then the psyche begins to apply it to the outer and inner Worlds resulting in a shift in perception. (Cordovero's Tree, 16th century)

Analysis

The mystery of Existence has always intrigued human beings. While plants and animals have instinctive and practical intelligence, only human beings appear to be capable of abstract consideration. Because each individual is a microcosmic image of Existence, we have the capacity to perceive the Divine Plan as we resonate with the macrocosm.

The design of the Tree comes into view with its central axis of equilibrium and the side pillars of the active and passive processes. The horizontal divisions define four levels within each World. The twenty-two paths generate not only the upper and lower faces of the Tree, as they are called, but also twelve triads plus seven vertical levels within the scheme. Together they set out the basic metaphysical system of Kabbalah.

The symbolic aspects of the Tree are seen in the Names of God, Divine functions such as Justice and Mercy, as well as in the archetypes of the biblical patriarchs. In kabbalistic astrology, the planets are ascribed to the sefirot and the zodiacal signs to the triads. The Tree can also be related to the anatomy of the psyche, the structure of a school of the soul or that of Evolution in scientific terms.

Jacob's Ladder is composed of four Trees that reveal how the Divine, Spirit, psyche and physicality interact. Crucial functions are seen in how the lower part of an upper Tree overlaps the upper part of a lower Tree. Most important are the places where the three upper Worlds and the three lower Worlds meet. This allows the psyche to observe the body as well as the spiritual and Divine dimensions. These connections may give a mystical experience in contemplation which is one of the aims of this practice.

Metaphysics

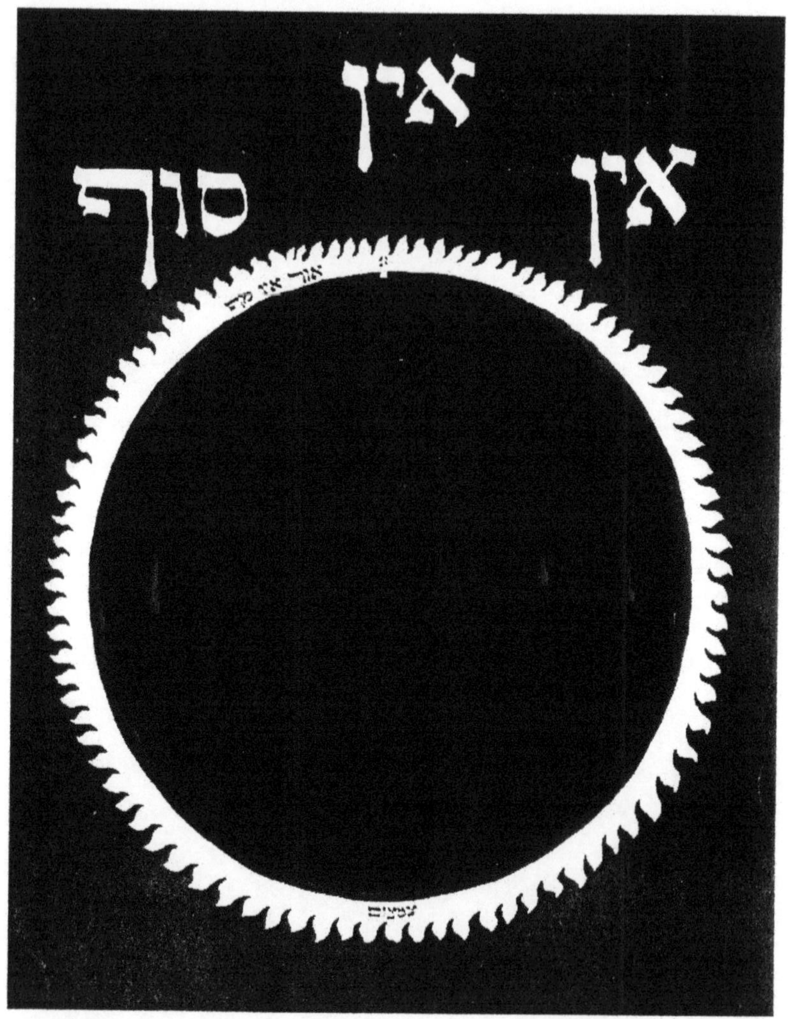

Figure 5—ORIGINS
Here the Hebrew words AYIN, Nothingness, and EN SOF, the Endless, hover beyond the sphere of EN SOF AUR, the Light of the Limitless. This circle of Light, representing the Will of God, surrounds the Void of unmanifest Existence. The Holy One generated the Zim Zum, or contraction, that brought this first dimension into being. This set the stage for manifestation to begin. (Drawing by Prof. James Russell, 20th century)

1. Origins

Before the beginning there was No-thing. God the Absolute is beyond Existence. According to the esoteric tradition, "God wished to behold God" or, as the Kabbalists put it, "Face did not gaze upon Face". Therefore 'Somethingness' had to be brought into being to reflect an image, symbolised in the biblical Holy Name EHYEH, I AM.

According to Kabbalah, the term used to define the Godhead is *Ayin* or Nothingness as well as its opposite, *En Sof*, meaning Endless. Together these two terms express what can not be described except in a philosophical abstraction or a symbolic form.

Out of this combination emerges the Will of God, represented by *En Sof Aur* or the Light of the Limitless. This pure Consciousness precipitates the first phenomena of manifestation. They are called the Three Hidden Lights, or *Zahzahot*, which correspond to the Yang, Yin and Tao in Chinese metaphysics and Rajas, Tamas and Sattva in the esoteric Hindu system. This Trinity becomes operational as the Void, generated by the Holy One's withdrawal, begins to manifest God's intention. The situation can be likened to an empty stage before a play begins.

This Void, which is at least 'somethingness', has a unique quality in that it will contain the Past, Present and Future in an Eternal Now. The rabbinic saying "God's place is the World, but the World is not God's place" reflects this mystery of Existence.

Figure 6—EMANATION

Here the first burst of radiation from the Godhead brings the Divine World into being. This expands to produce a vast blossom that eventually, after reaching its limit, will return to its point of origin and disappear back into Nothingness again. A parallel is the physical Big Bang at the beginning of the material level, the last of the four Worlds of Emanation, Creation, Formation and Action that compose Existence. (Robert Fludd, 17th century)

2. *Emanation*

The term 'emanation' is related to fire, the radiant element. This allows an insight into the most subtle and potent aspect of Existence, that all 'things' are the result of this first Divine manifestation. If this realm of pure consciousness should be withdrawn back to the Absolute, then Existence would disappear like the radiance of a lamp when it is switched off. A parallel is seen at the moment of death when the light of life fades from the eyes as the dying person passes away into a higher, invisible World. Existence will continue only as long as the Light of the Absolute is present within it.

At this initial point in the Divine process, the Void was quite empty, like a hollow within a ball that is sometimes called 'Negative Existence'. As yet, there was nothing present within it except possibilities. This Divine Void is still present as a background to every event in the hidden stillness behind all manifestation.

At some moment decided by the Absolute, the *Kav* or Line of Divine Will penetrated the periphery of the Void. This juncture is called Keter, the hollow Crown at the head of the sefirotic Tree through which God's Will is extended to fill the Void.

According to kabbalistic tradition, this situation will continue until the End of Time, when all that has been conceived is fulfilled in a great Cosmic Cycle. On the last Day of Existence, everything that has come into being will be assessed according to its performance. Kabbalah says there are ten such great cycles. These correspond to the Hindu idea of universal seasons that symbolise the birth, flowering, withering and death of a chain of Worlds. The physical universe is but the lowest rung of what Kabbalah calls Jacob's Ladder.

Figure 7—SEFIROT
Within the sphere of the Light of the Limitless emerge ten Divine Attributes that set out the Laws of Existence. These Laws are eternal and underlie all that was, is and shall be, until the End of Time. Here is the framework for the Holy Name I AM THAT I AM in which the first I AM may behold the second I AM in the THAT of the Mirror of Existence. (Drawing by Prof. James Russell, 20th century)

3. *Azilut*

The Hebrew word Azilut means "to be next to", which defines the relationship between God and Existence. This first World of Emanation is not God but an expression of the Holy One's Will. As such, it both reveals and conceals the Godhead. Azilut is also called the Garment of God. Some mystics call it the Garden of Holy Apples.

Keter, the first and highest sefirah of Azilut, already contains all the sefirot before they are separated and organised into different levels and functions. A parallel is a seed that contains within it the whole tree which will grow according to a preconceived plan and specific laws. Even the death and the end of an oak are present in an acorn.

One may consider the Keter of Azilut as the seed of all Existence. In this case, the Tree and later Jacob's Ladder grow down in order to allow the return impulse of ascent in cosmic and human evolution.

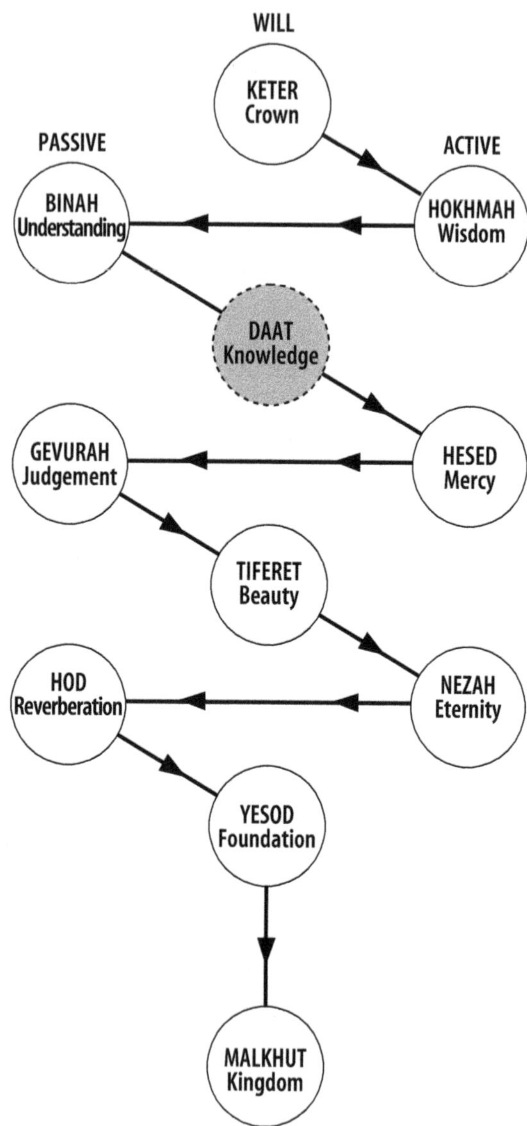

Figure 8—DESCENT
This is the descending order of the sefirot that sets out various levels and functions of the Tree of Life. The Will of the Holy One holds the equilibrium between the active and passive principles of Existence. (Halevi)

4. Lightning Flash

Once the enormous potential held in the Keter of Azilut is set in motion by the Will of God, it follows a path called the Lightning Flash. It zigzags between the three pillars or principles of equilibrium, active and passive or neutral, positive and negative, which echo the three Hidden Lights of Zahzahot beyond manifestation.

The discharge of the Lightning Flash unfolds the sefirot in a distinct sequence. Hokhmah, the next sefirah after Keter to emerge, carries a positive charge which seeks balance in Binah on the opposite side. The zigzag then continues further down and comes to a momentary equilibrium at the first interval of Daat where the process pauses to reflect on what is above before continuing towards the active side. Daat is also called a non-sefirah that veils the supernal sefirot from those to emerge below.

The Lightning Flash then proceeds from Hesed to the opposite side of Gevurah, before reaching the central position of equilibrium at Tiferet. The Lightning Flash then proceeds zigzagging down to the active sefirah of Nezah and then the passive Hod, before coming to equilibrium at Yesod. This is the second interval where the process pauses before being finally resolved at Malkhut.

This process also sets out the other paths between the sefirot which brings the triads of the system into being. This generates an ascending Lightning Flash between what is below and above. Once the sefirot, paths and triads are in place, the symbol of the Tree of Life is complete to become the master blueprint of all Existence that is to follow.

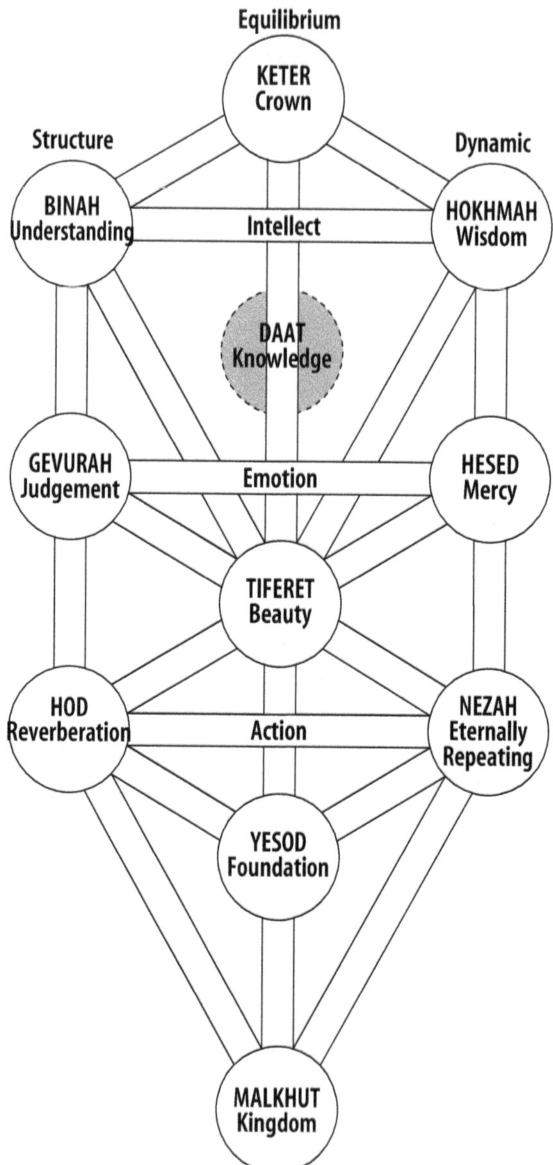

Figure 9—SEFIROTIC PRINCIPLES
The word sefirot means "numbers". They are also seen as Divine Attributes, their traditional names giving an insight into their functions. The Tree of Life diagram first came into public domain in medieval Spain. (Halevi)

5. *Tree of Life*

Once the Lightning Flash has completed its descent, the World of Azilut is organised into a set of metaphysical laws known as the Tree of Life. Composed of ten sefirot plus the non-sefirah of Daat, three pillars, twenty-two paths and twelve triads, it is to be the model of all beings and processes in Existence.

The two side pillars govern the dynamic and structural sefirot, whereas those on the central pillar represent a balancing principle. Through the central column of consciousness God has access to every level in Existence. It is said that will is consciousness in action.

The three horizontal paths define the levels of Action, Emotion and Intellect. The topmost triad below Keter is concerned with the radiance of Divinity. These four aspects of the Tree also relate to the elements of Earth, Water, Air and Fire.

The Tree is an integrated system where nothing works in isolation. The paths, for example, connect the sefirot which allows communication to flow in many directions. Thus an event in one part of the Tree may affect the whole process. The paths also define the various triads which have more specific functions.

The kite-like configurations, the upper and the lower faces of the Tree, are sometimes called the Divine Countenance and Beard of the Ancient One. The upper is seen as masculine and the lower one as feminine, reflecting the polarity between the active and passive principles. The two side pillars are regarded as the limbs of a vast humanoid figure, Adam Kadmon.

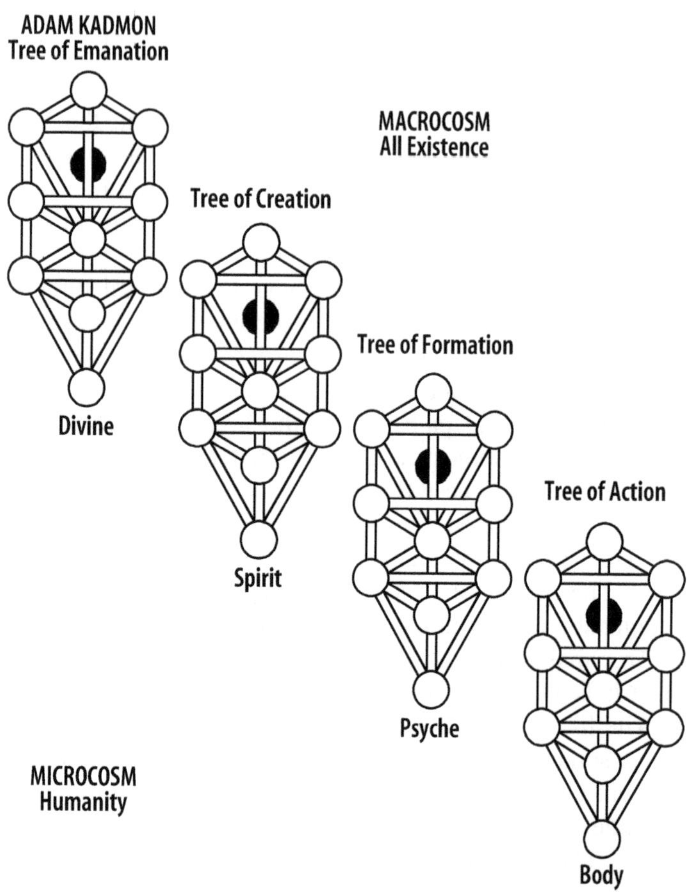

Figure 10—MANIFESTATION
Here the four Worlds are depicted separately so as to define their distinct qualities and functions. Each Tree is a different order of reality. These four Worlds do, however, operate as an integrated and unified system. The precision of kabbalistic metaphysics complements the symbolism of myths, legends and visions. (Halevi)

6. Four Worlds

The esoteric view of Existence takes into account the macrocosmic metaphysical scheme that has three other Worlds besides the physical universe. While each one obeys the archetypal laws of the sefirotic Tree, they are quite distinct realities.

In the process of descent, the Tiferet of a higher World becomes the source or Keter of a lower World. The Yesod of a higher World underlies the Daat of a lower World, while the Malkhut of a higher World coincides with the Tiferet of a lower World. This fundamental interconnection allows all four Trees to operate as an integrated system called Jacob's Ladder.

The World of Emanation (Azilut) is the origin which contains everything that was, is and shall be in Eternity. The 'Divine spark' within a human being resides there. Time begins in the dynamic World of Creation (Beriah) where the essence of every created entity comes into being. The human spirit belongs to this World.

The World of Formation (Yezirah) is also called Paradise where spiritual essences acquire distinct forms. The human psyche resonates with this level of Existence. The lowest World of Action (Asiyyah) represents the physical universe as well as the human body. Here Time takes on a material dimension when all created and formed entities come into manifestation in a preordained sequence as Creation begins the return journey of Evolution.

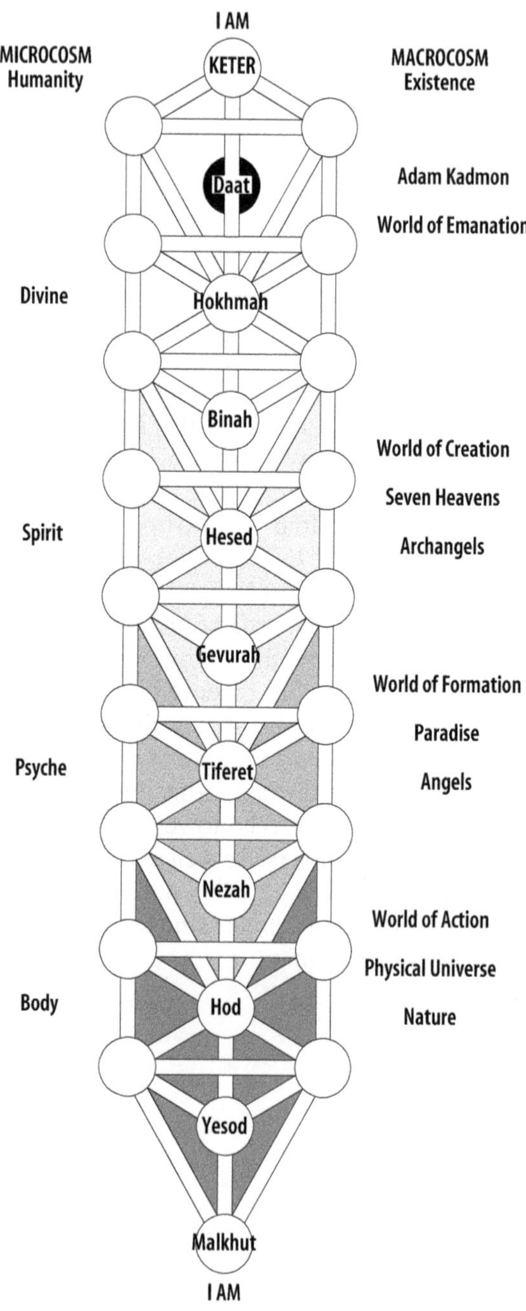
I AM
MICROCOSM
Humanity
KETER
MACROCOSM
Existence
Daat
Adam Kadmon
World of Emanation
Divine
Hokhmah
Binah
World of Creation
Seven Heavens
Spirit
Hesed
Archangels
Gevurah
World of Formation
Paradise
Psyche
Tiferet
Angels
Nezah
World of Action
Physical Universe
Body
Hod
Nature
Yesod
Malkhut
I AM

7. Jacob's Ladder

The integrated system of the four Worlds is called Jacob's Ladder. Its hallmark is the vertical fifth Tree on the central column of consciousness. This Great Tree locks all the rungs into interactive levels. Through this central axis, God is present in all the Worlds from the highest Keter to the lowest Malkhut.

The interaction between the Worlds is possible because the upper face of a lower Tree overlays the lower face of a higher Tree, indicating that they can operate at the same level from different realities. The junctions where three Worlds meet are crucially important. The higher one at the Keter of Yezirah coincides with the Tiferet of Beriah and the Malkhut of Azilut, also called the Kingdom of God. The lower junction combines the Keter of Asiyyah, the Tiferet of Yezirah and the Malkhut of Beriah, which is called the Kingdom of Heaven. This lower focus corresponds to the Self of a human psyche, whereas the higher one grants direct access to the Divine.

Humanity was positioned in the physical universe after all other inhabitants of the Ladder were in place. The archangels reside in the seven Heavens while the angels belong to Paradise. In this scheme, the planets of our Solar system are seen as angelic entities whereas the Sun is regarded as an archangelic being.

It took millions of years to arrive at a point where organic life on the planet Earth became possible. From here on began the process of Self-conscious evolution on the 'Return' journey to the Divine source of Existence and the fulfilment of its purpose.

Figure 11—CHAIN OF BEING (Left)

This kabbalistic scheme was not in the public domain because it was considered too complex for those without esoteric knowledge. However, some texts speak of a series of nuts within shells which stretch between the Godhead and the Earth. There are hints of a Ladder of Ascension in rabbinic texts such as the Hekalot, which describes the various levels of Earth, Paradise and Heaven. (Halevi)

Symbolism

Figure 12—KAVOD
One of the symbols used to describe Azilut is the Kavod or the Glory. In this calligraphy, the Divine Name YHVH is written vertically in the form of a humanoid figure, the radiant image of Adam Kadmon. This outline of a Divine Self-portrait is to be the model for humanity's Self-realisation. (Halevi)

8. Adam Kadmon

In contrast to the metaphysical exposition of the Tree of Life, there is the symbolic approach. This is seen in the arts of every culture be they visual, musical or poetic. Symbolism is an emotional rather than an intellectual way of describing aspects of Existence. Here, an artistic rendering of YHVH is made up of four Hebrew letters, YOD, HE, VAV and HE. This presentation of the sacred name in vertical mode defines the composition of Adam Kadmon.

The first letter YOD represents the head. Its form is a flame symbolising the Divine fire that enlightens the mind. The upper letter HE depicts the shoulders, chest and arms, while the lower HE outlines the hips and legs. Together they define the levels of emotion and action, while the arms and legs also represent the active and passive side pillars. The letter VAV in the middle can be seen as the heart and spine on the central pillar of consciousness.

According to tradition, each human being originates from a specific part of the primordial Adam's body. That will give a particular quality to the individual's destiny through many incarnations. For example, a scientist may come from the brain of Adam Kadmon while the hand may generate a talent in art.

This figure is composed of 'white fire' in contrast to the 'black fire' of the background, which is the all-pervading but invisible presence of the Absolute. A symbol like a spire can represent the holy mountain while the Menorah is a reminder of Divinity.

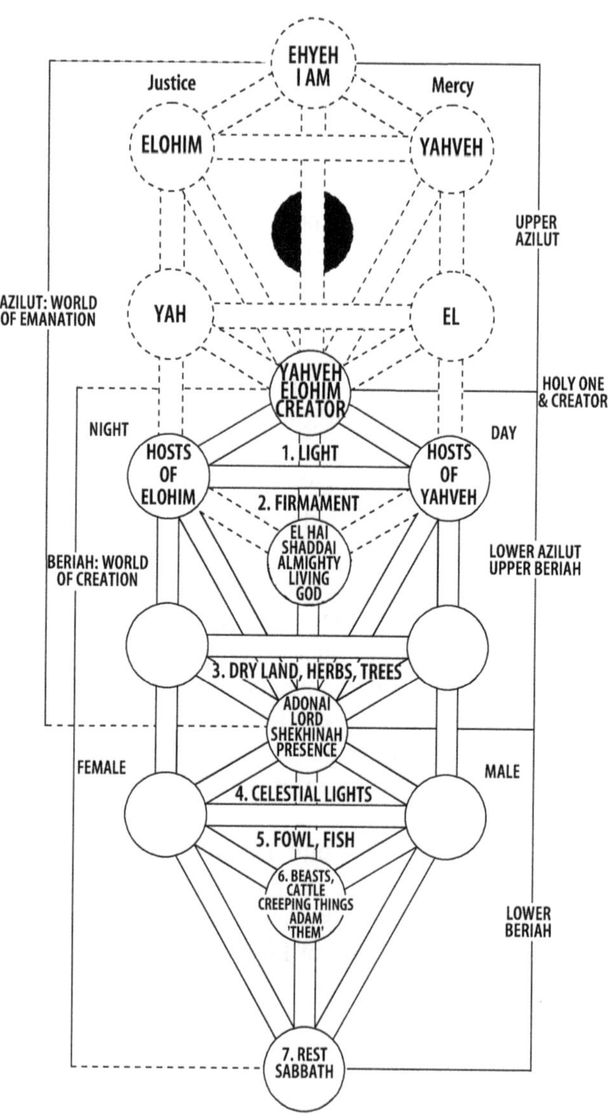

Figure 13—SEPARATION
Creation or Beriah corresponds to Plato's World of Ideas that emerges from the World of Emanation or Azilut. The seven days of Creation are seen here in the seven levels of the central pillar. These describe in poetic terms the philosophical basis of this second World of Jacob's Ladder. (Halevi)

9. *Extension*

The Tree of Creation emerges from the World of Eternity as potentiality moves towards actualisation. While the lower World is in movement, the Eternal Now holds it in place as long as the Absolute wills it.

The holy names given in the Bible are associated with the sefirot of Azilut. The Divine statement EHYEH—I AM at Keter is the primordial source of all. YAHVEH means I WILL BE, while ELOHIM can be translated as the MANY aspects of Divinity. EL and YAH define the level of Divine Mercy and Justice, while the CREATOR at Tiferet combines the upper face of Azilut in the name YAHVEH-ELOHIM. Thus when the Holy One initiates Creation, that place will become the Keter/Crown of Beriah.

The lower face of Azilut underlies the upper face of the World of Creation. Thus the HOSTS OF YAHVEH and HOSTS OF ELOHIM, EL HAI SHADDAI—THE LIVING ALMIGHTY and ADONAI—MY LORD are the hidden dimensions that support the process of separation between Eternity and Time. Here the essences of all that are to manifest in the lower Worlds are created into a sequential order.

As the Great Lightning Flash descends, so the lower face of Beriah separates from the Divine World of unity. With this comes the possibility of imperfection as the process comes under more complex laws and variations.

Figure 14—GENESIS

In the Bible, the seven Days of Creation describe the unfolding of the spiritual realm. The Days can be seen as vast archetypal cosmic processes. This is the World of essences, as yet without form, also called the Heavens. (Rev. T.Bankes's Bible, 19th century)

10. Creation

The Bible begins with the seven Days of Creation. The World of Emanation was part of the esoteric oral tradition that was considered too subtle and sacred for the public domain. It was only given to the Elders of Israel as such potent knowledge could be misunderstood by the Children of Israel or younger souls.

When God said, "Let there be light", this was the emergence of Emanation illuminating the darkness of the as yet vacant void of Existence. On the second Day, the dimensions of above and below came into being with the creation of the firmament. On the third Day, the elemental archetypes of water and earth were created as well as the spirits of all plants, that is, the principle of organic life. The celestial lights created on the fourth Day were quite different from that of Emanation on the first Day. They were either radiant or reflective entities as the universe became increasingly differentiated. The cosmic space was ready for inhabitants to occupy it.

On the fifth Day, the fowl of the air and the fish of the sea symbolise the celestial orders of archangels and angels. On the sixth Day, the spirits of the terrestrial creatures manifested as the beasts of the field. The spiritual Adam was the last being to be created. "Male and female created He them." On the seventh Day of Shabbat, the process came to rest as the World of Beriah was now complete.

This order of great hierarchy was recognised by most esoteric traditions. While the angelics were regarded as gods and even demons, the universe was seen as a cosmic cycle of integration and disintegration, like birth and death.

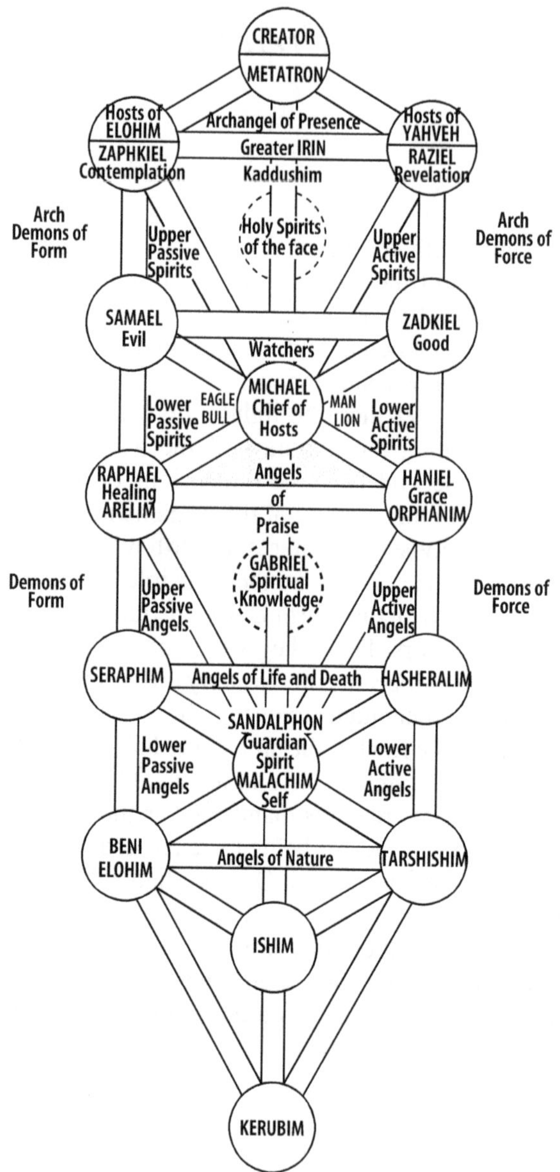

Figure 15—ANGELICS
These celestial creatures have the function of managing the various processes of Existence. By maintaining the vast order of the cosmos, they aid humanity to realise its potential. Angelics are the servants of God, whereas humans are the children of God. (Halevi)

11. Celestial Order

Every spiritual tradition recognises that there are celestial non-human beings called angelics. The Merkabah tradition contributed much to what is known about them and the rabbis organised the information into a hierarchy likened to a well-organised Roman army with its various ranks.

The World of Creation is the domain of the archangels. Their names give a clue to their functions, the '-el' indicating that they are the servants of God. Michael means "Like unto God" and his task at the Tiferet of Beriah is to be the Captain of the Hosts of Heaven, while Gabriel means the "Warrior of God". The archangels between the left and right pillars hold the balance between order and chaos.

The arts usually depict the angelics in a human form but with wings, indicating they are not terrestrial creatures. However, although they can manifest in such a form, they are cosmic principles relating to their sefirotic functions. Although very powerful beings, they are limited to their particular area.

In contrast Metatron, the first fully Self-realised human being Enoch, was taken up to the highest Heaven and given archangelic powers. He is closer to the Creator than any angelic. His task is to watch over humanity. He is manifest as Sandalfon at the Malkhut of Beriah, or the Kingdom of Heaven, where he collects genuine prayers and presents them to the Holy One.

The angels who inhabit the World of Yezirah compose the lesser ranks of the celestial chain of command. Their scope of action is more specialised as they are concerned with maintaining particular functions. Below the angels come the terrestrial Nature spirits who are the dynamic workforce of organic life.

Figure 16—EDEN
The Garden of Eden is a symbol of the World of Forms, or Yezirah. The Tree of Life above represents the Divine World, whereas the Tree of Knowledge is the archetype of the World of Creation. Paradise is also called the Treasure House of Souls where Adam and Eve resided prior to the Fall. (Medieval woodcut)

12. Paradise

After the seven Days of Creation, the Bible story moves on to the Garden of Eden. This corresponds to Plato's World of Forms. There, for example, the idea of a rose manifests in different forms of roses. Paradise is always described as a most beautiful place, "pleasant to the sight" as the Bible puts it.

In the World of Yezirah, the androgynous spirit of Adam was divided into male and female souls, Adam and Eve. They were in a state of innocence, that is, without any experience when they arrived in the Garden of Eden. There they had everything they needed at that point.

However, God had given them one commandment, "not to eat of the Tree of the Knowledge of Good and Evil". According to the legend, the serpent who tempted Adam and Eve was Lucifer who had fallen from grace and was envious of humans. The couple accepted Lucifer's suggestion to taste the forbidden fruit. When they did, their eyes opened and they became aware of possibilities that they were not ready for.

That was their first lesson of temptation and its consequences when they chose to break the Divine commandment. While God had anticipated this, Adam and Eve had only themselves to blame when they were driven out of Eden. God made them "garments of skin", that is, they had to incarnate into physical bodies.

Humanity is quite different from any other creature with the potential of full consciousness and Self-realisation. The development was to be a slow process, over many incarnations, but between lives humans would return to the appropriate level of Paradise, also called the Treasure House of Souls, for rest and reflection.

Many myths of various traditions speak of an idyllic Golden Age in a distant past. That is an allegory of the time in Paradise before humanity descended to into physicality.

Figure 17—RELATIVITY
This image is one of the first human formulations about the organisation of the universe within a geocentric system. Held aloft by an Hellenic angelic known as Atlas, it encompassed all the observable stars, the Zodiac, the solar system and the terrestrial elements. Here was one of the first scientific theories of relativity. What lay beyond was theology. (Woodcut, 16th century)

13. Materiality

The question, 'How did Existence begin?' has always fascinated human beings. Indeed, every tradition has its own creation myth. As modern science started to replace religion, it was still faced with the same ultimate question.

According to current scientific theory, the physical universe came into being in what is called the Big Bang that began as a brilliant point, seemingly appearing out of nothingness. In that moment all space, time, energy and matter came into manifestation. The first phase was composed of waves and particles which produced the gases hydrogen and helium that over millions of years generated galaxies, stars and the elemental universe as it is now in time.

The material universe can be seen in terms of four states of matter: solids, liquids, gases and radiance. They exist at the lowest Malkhut of Jacob's Ladder. There they interact with each other in different combinations. Out of this came a situation in which organic life could appear on earth.

Science has different theories about the future of the material universe. The view that predicts expansion of the cosmos and then contraction back to the point where it started is close to the esoteric tradition. As there was a beginning, so there must also be an End of Time. In Kabbalah, this process is known as a *Shemittah* or a great cosmic cycle.

Figure 18—CHARIOT

Before the development of philosophy, symbolism was the language used to describe the higher Worlds. For example, Ezekiel's vision revealed the fourfold structure of Existence. As such, it became the source of much speculation and later the model for the Merkabah or 'Chariot' tradition of Jewish mystics. (The Bear Bible, 16th century)

14. Vision

While in exile in the land of Chaldeans, the biblical prophet Ezekiel had an extraordinary vision as he sat by the river Chebar. He described it in great detail and its symbolism can be seen as an archetypal model of the higher Worlds.

Ezekiel saw in his revelation the appearance of four living creatures, each with four wings and the faces of a man, a lion, an ox and an eagle. They can be seen as the four levels within Existence. These four angelics each had a wheel that had wheels within and eyes on their rims. These wheels represent the cosmic cycles that govern the universe under the command of these higher intelligences.

Over the heads of these angelics appeared the likeness of a firmament, which defines the division between the Worlds of Yezirah and Beriah. Above was a Throne upon which sat a likeness of a human being. The throne symbolises Heaven while the fiery man represents the Glory of God, also known as Adam Kadmon.

Ezekiel described the Glory as having the appearance of great luminosity. There was, however, a difference in the quality of light in the upper and lower body. In terms of Jacob's Ladder, the upper part of Adam Kadmon is in the World of Azilut while the lower part overlaps with the realm of Beriah below.

While Ezekiel's vision came to him spontaneously, later mystics called Chariot Riders tried to achieve a similar vision by personal effort. In their meditation technique they used the inner chariot of the psyche whereby they could ascend to the level of the spirit, the domain of Heaven, and so glimpse the Glory of God.

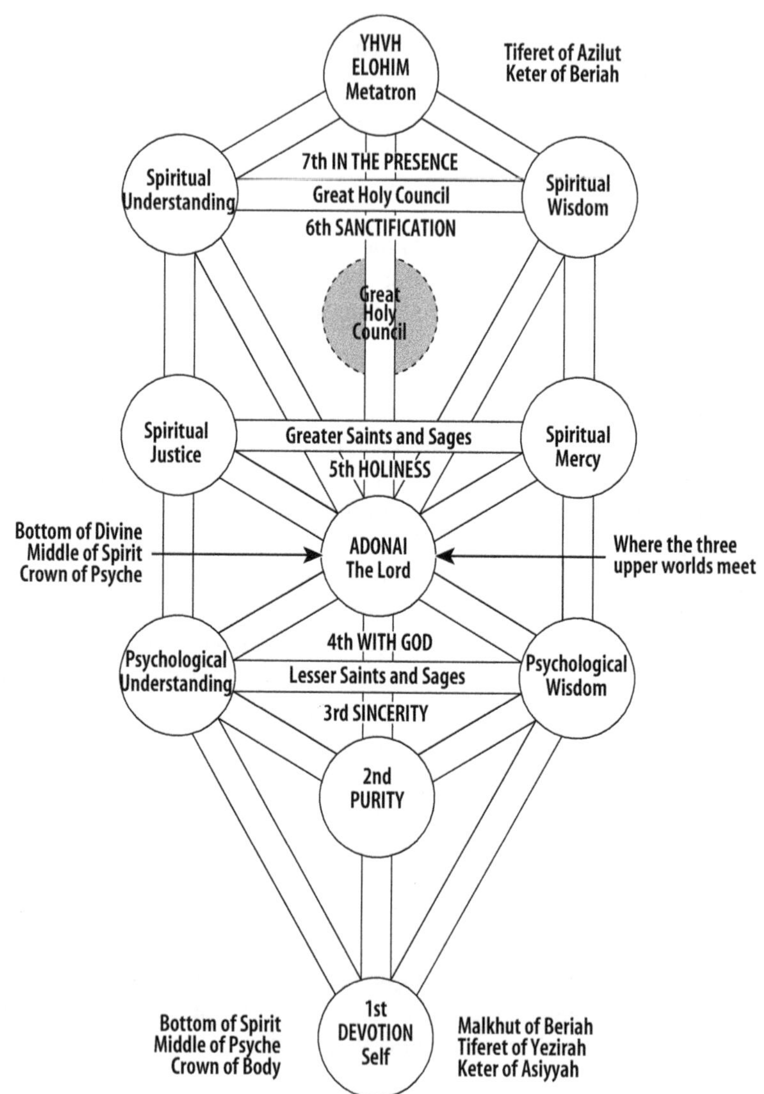

Figure 19—ASCENT

Many esoteric traditions recognise an ascending order of spiritual levels. According to Kabbalah, there are seven Heavens each with a distinct quality. One needs to be well balanced before attempting to climb the Holy Mountain. If one is permitted to enter the Heavenly Halls, then there is assistance from inner teachers, saints and sages who know the Way. (Halevi)

15. Heavenly Halls

An experience of the Heavenly Halls is in essence indescribable. However, people try to explain what they "see" but such descriptions are transmitted through a particular person's psyche which is influenced by cultural conditioning. For example, a Buddhist might see Bodhisattvas while a Jew or a Christian perceives angels, saints and sages. Not all experiences are visual. They can be a sense of space, sound or otherworldly fragrances. The hallmark is 'awesome'. According to tradition, there are seven Heavens or levels of spirituality. They are the domain of what some call the Greater Mysteries.

In Kabbalah, the first Hall is called the Kingdom of Heaven. True 'Devotion' is needed to enter this transpersonal dimension. The quality of the second Heaven is said to be 'Purity' which can be perceived through the Daat of the psyche. The Hall of 'Sincerity' or the third Heaven coincides with the higher intellect level of Hokhmah and Binah of the psyche. One is said to be 'with God' in the fourth Heaven which touches the lowest sefirah of the Divine Realm. This is the place of the Heavenly Jerusalem where one may have visions of its inhabitants and even have discussions with them.

The fifth Heaven is described as 'Holiness'. It is much sought after because of its blissful quality and detachment from the psychological World. The sixth Heaven is called the place of 'Sanctification' where the Hosts of Heaven praise God. Here also is the domain of the Great Holy Council who administer Providence. The seventh Heaven 'in the Presence' of the Creator is the Divine level of Beriah where one may glimpse the archangel Enoch/Metatron at the head of the human hierarchy.

It is said that the angelics are envious of human beings and will try to stop an individual who is not worthy from ascending to the higher Worlds. Only those of purity and integrity are allowed to proceed.

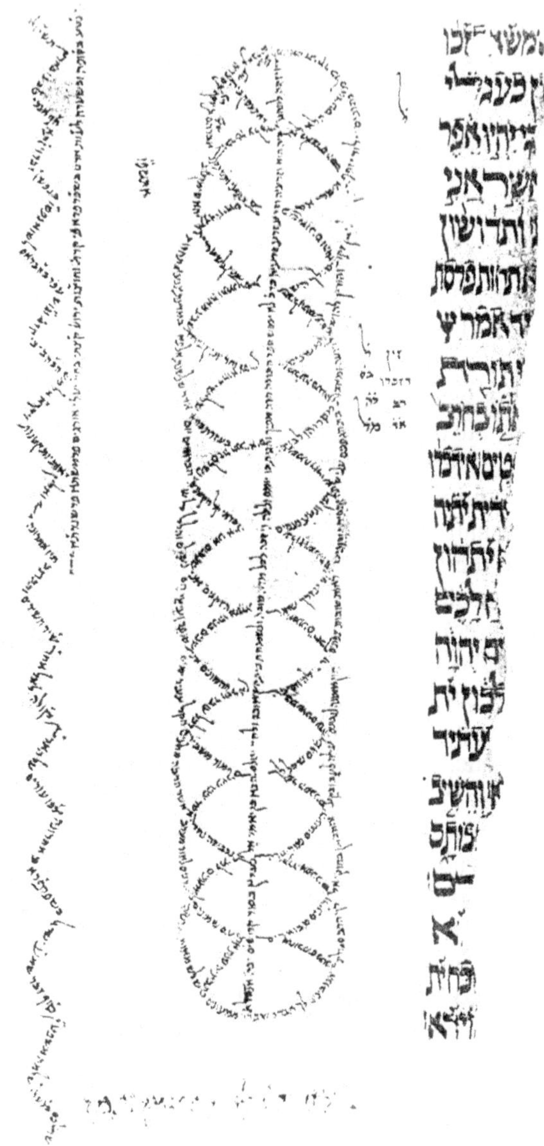

Figure 20—ESOTERIC

It can be assumed that the scribe who produced this calligraphy belonged to a school of the soul. He used an exoteric text to hint at the Great Chain of Being in this configuration. During the medieval period, esoteric ideas often had to be concealed. They were only recognised by "those who know". (Yemeni manuscript, 15th century)

16. Lineage

There is much folklore to complement the biblical stories. According to a Jewish legend, when Adam and Eve were cast out of Eden, God sent the archangel Raziel, whose name means 'the Secrets of God', to give them a book. That book contained instructions for the return journey, that is, esoteric knowledge about human development and the purpose of Existence.

In the long process of evolution, an oral tradition accumulated into a body of knowledge which was transmitted by word of mouth through generations. It was based on metaphysical thought and observation as well as revelation coming down the vertical line of the *Kav* or Divine Will that is present throughout Jacob's Ladder from top to bottom.

By the time of Abraham, the written tradition was already well established. He came from Ur of the Chaldees which by then was a civilised city with a temple and a university as well as much cultural interaction due to its international commerce. Trade routes were important not only for transporting goods but also books, new ideas and inventions to distant places. Abraham learnt to read and write there as well as absorbing various belief systems.

Abraham's initiation by Melchizedek at the site of the future Jerusalem was the beginning of the three monotheistic religions which gave rise to many esoteric lines handed down until today. This was the result of many committed individuals and groups refining and adapting the tradition for each period. Later the encounter with Greek metaphysics and philosophy in the Middle Ages brought about a synthesis of reason and revelation. Even today, the blend of modern science and psychology is beginning to bring about a more profound comprehension of Existence.

Earth

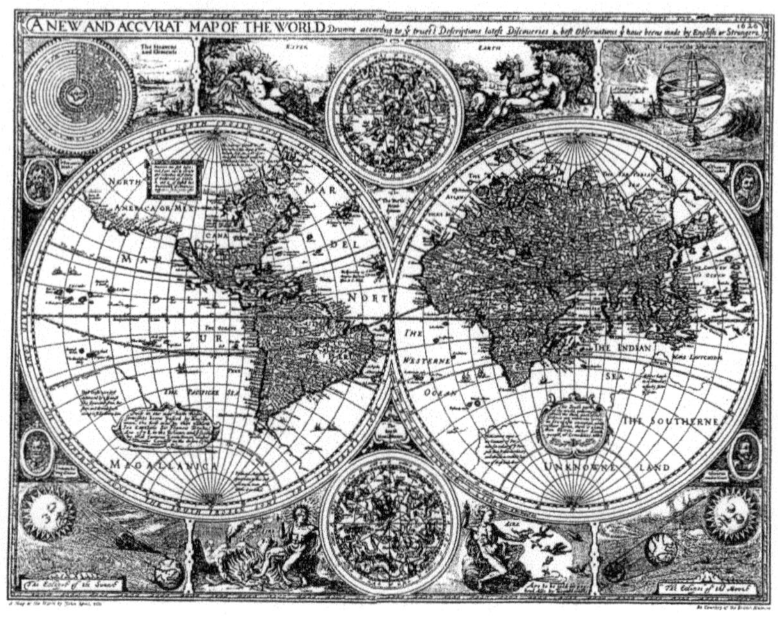

Figure 21—PLANET

Mother Earth has not always looked like this. When she was young, she was not even solid. In her adulthood, she changes appearance according to annual seasons as well as cosmic epochs of ice ages and tropical periods. Continents move slowly to new positions and coastlines change rapidly with rising sea levels. In her old age, she will shrivel and die. (16th century print)

17. Mother Earth

When human beings first descended from the Treasure House of Souls they had to adjust to the terrestrial environment. Earth provided what they needed for physical survival but human beings also wanted to make sense of their position.

At first, humanity was only aware of its immediate locality. Over time, as people spread and migrated across the globe, the scale of distance also expanded in the collective experience and memory. At first the Earth appeared to be basically flat wherever they were, despite the seas and mountains. For a long time, the world view was geocentric. Later the heliocentric view defined the Earth's place amongst the other planets that orbit the Sun.

Now it is known that our particular Solar system is just a tiny part of the galaxy called the Milky Way. Moreover, there are myriads of such stellar clusters of galaxies. And yet, in the vastness of this universe, our Earth seems to be unique in its ability to sustain organic life and consciousness at this point in time. No extraterrestrial creature, up to this moment in history, has presented itself to mankind although we are now on the lookout.

The ancients revered Mother Earth as a goddess or an angelic being. The old concept of 'Gaia' has re-emerged out of the modern scientific view, that is, seeing the Earth as an intelligent living entity. As such, it has a specific cosmic purpose within the Divine Plan.

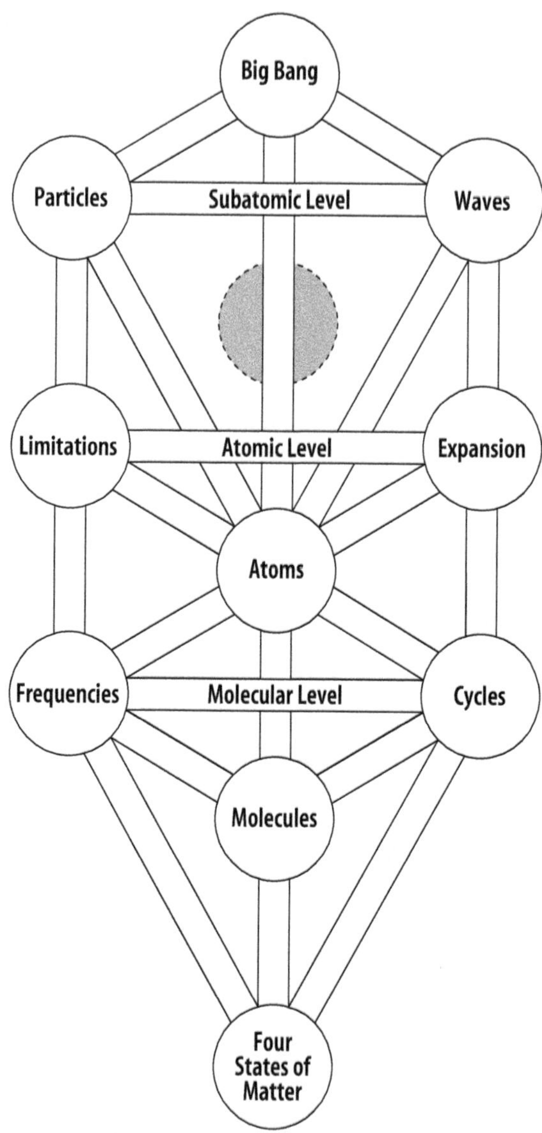

Figure 22—MATERIALITY

When the physical universe came into being, the patterns and laws of Creation and Formation were already in place. The process followed the Lightning Flash path between the pillars of dynamic and structure as it came down through various levels. The central pillar of equilibrium, that is, the Divine principle of the Kav, holds all the Worlds together. (Halevi)

18. Building Blocks

Most of the physical World is too subtle for human sense perception. New scientific instruments can measure some invisible levels while esoteric traditions have taken them into account in their metaphysics.

The radiant emanation of the Big Bang at Keter brought the principles of waves and particles into being at the Hokhmah and Binah level of materiality. The expansion of the process at Hesed on this scale produced variable environments while the principle of limitation at Gevurah gave rise to differentiation. The particles either attracted or repelled each other, coming together as atoms at Tiferet.

An atom is the essence of a particular element. New ones are still being discovered and added to the Periodic Table of Elements. These are found not only in our Earth and Solar system but throughout the physical universe.

Waves, particles and atoms are constantly moving which can be likened to Shiva's dance in Indian mythology. Their cycles and frequencies, representing Nezah and Hod, form many new combinations called molecules that relate to the sefirah of Yesod, the Foundation. These minute building blocks of the physical World become organised over time into four states of matter at Malkhut. Here we perceive them as solids, liquids, gases and radiance.

Although solid matter appears to be dense, most of it is composed of space. Some traditions say that matter is only an illusion. However, it has its own reality in physical Existence. The World of Action is the place for evolution and development which would not occur in the World of Forms or Paradise.

Figure 23—ELEMENTS
Fingal's Cave, off the western coast of Scotland, is an example of elemental interaction. It was produced by fiery volcanic eruptions, atmospheric conditions and oceanic rhythms over a very long time. The result was this unique rock formation. (19th century print)

19. Mineral Kingdom

The mineral level of the Earth had once started as the simplest elements of hydrogen and helium. Now there is an abundance of inorganic life on the planet.

Although minerals and metals appear to be inert, they are in a process of continuous transformation in their own timescale of millions of years. The Earth is like a chemical retort. Its rocks rise, sink and crumble under intense interior heat and pressure as well as the exterior pressures from the Sun, Moon and planets.

Climate and weather conditions play a crucial role in the life cycle of minerals. Erosion grinds down the highest mountains into fragments which in turn become part of new compounds while water and wind can turn even sand to dust. Meanwhile, some minerals grow into particular shapes known as crystals when conditions are right.

Humanity has refined the mineral kingdom further by transforming it into utensils and works of art. Some precious stones and metals like diamonds and gold are highly valued as prestige symbols. The practical application shifts the mineral's level of being as its function changes from passive to active.

Certain rocks and mountains have a strong presence which people have recognised throughout the ages and regarded them as sacred. Individuals seek out deserts and mountains to find spiritual experience in the vastness of a transpersonal landscape. In a state of heightened consciousness, a mystic can perceive the Divine radiance permeating every stone and pebble. "Split a stone and I am there."

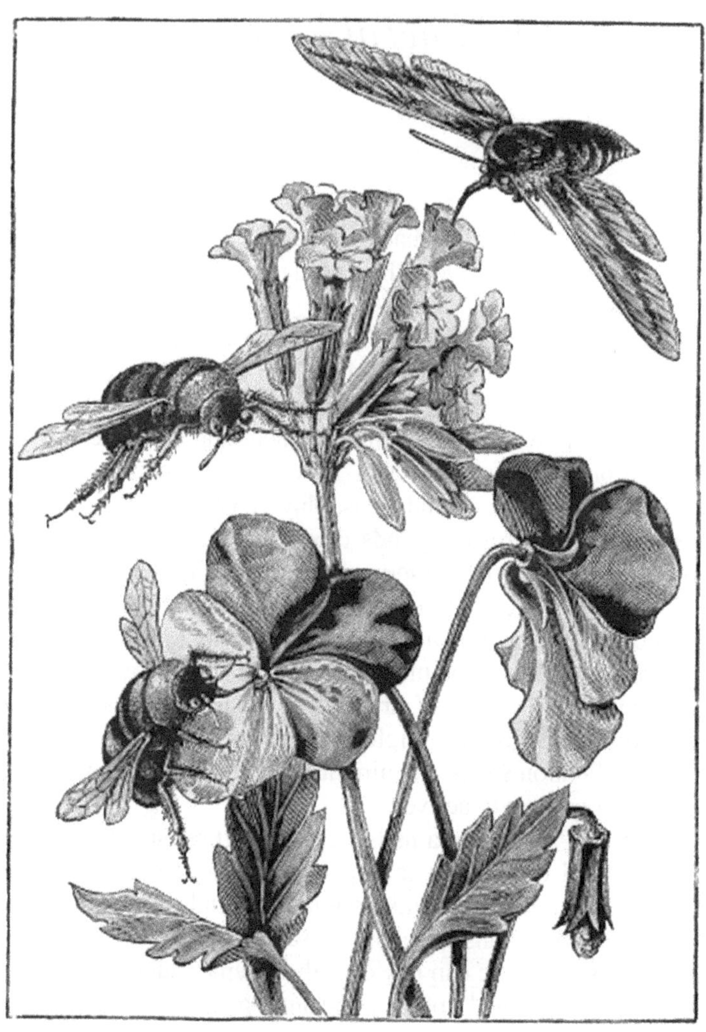

Figure 24—PLANTS
The reproduction and survival of the species is a great driving force of the vegetable kingdom. The more advanced plants have not only developed male and female flowers but also trade with animals, offering nectar for pollinating their flowers and fruit for distributing their seeds. (19th century print)

20. Vegetable Kingdom

The vegetable kingdom adds a new layer of consciousness and sensitivity to the planet. While minerals and metals can interact, they can not grow or reproduce. Those activities are the hallmark of organic life.

Every spring, a new cycle of growth appears seemingly out of nowhere when the plants respond to a cosmic impulse of the season. The four elements earth, water, air and fire are organised into myriads of different forms. The leaves and flowers often look like the Tree of Life in miniature in their symmetry of the left and right around a central vein, or pillar, as such patterns come down through all the Worlds into manifestation. Each species has its Yeziratic blueprint which is faithfully replicated, with small variations according to local circumstance.

In an apparently peaceful landscape, a big battle is going on as plants compete for their share of nourishment and light. The driving force is to produce the next generation. Although not all will achieve this, the abundance of flowers and seeds secures the survival of the species. Plants are largely at the mercy of external circumstances as they cannot move but they can adapt to their environment within limits. It is said that plants respond even to human influence and thrive if they are loved or go into shock if they are threatened.

The most striking feature of vegetation is the colour green. Photosynthesis uses the energy in sunlight to produce food for the plant itself and, incidentally, for other creatures. Thus we can consider the vegetable kingdom either from a practical point of view or study the organisation and beauty of various plants. And yet, it is said that what we see on Earth is dull compared with the original forms in Paradise.

Figure 25—TIGER

The ability to swim, crawl or walk is a big step on the road of Evolution. The tiger is an advanced form of animal, a warm-blooded mammal. Its body is composed of mineral and vegetable processes, but it also has a vital soul of instinctive intelligence with the accumulated experience of countless generations. (19th century print)

21. Animal Kingdom

Animal development began in water. It took on many forms from single-celled organisms to more complex creatures, the vertebrates. The ancestors of today's fish arrived around 400 million years ago. Later, reptilian amphibians took to the shore and developed limbs.

Then came the first species that were fully adapted to life on land. Many of the early forms, like the dinosaurs, are now extinct but there are still plenty of snakes and lizards with us. Some reptiles acquired the ability to fly, becoming the ancestors of today's birds.

The warm-blooded mammals are at the top of the animal hierarchy but even they carry the primordial sea in their body fluids. Although they have a freedom of movement that plants do not have, they are just as dependent on the four elements for their survival.

A sophisticated nervous system is a new phase of development. Higher animals are acutely aware of their surroundings and without doubt have both memory and intelligence. They teach their young the basic skills of life as well as being capable of play and crime. Even plants are competitive but animals can act out the impulse of being a 'top dog' and they are prepared to fight for their position. The herd instinct, on the other hand, relies on the law of large numbers in securing the continuity of the species and can be seen as the vegetable level of the animal kingdom.

Each species has its archetype in the higher Worlds. Animals may develop some degree of personality but they do not have individual souls like humans. When an animal dies, its particular experience goes back to the collective memory of the species and helps Evolution move on.

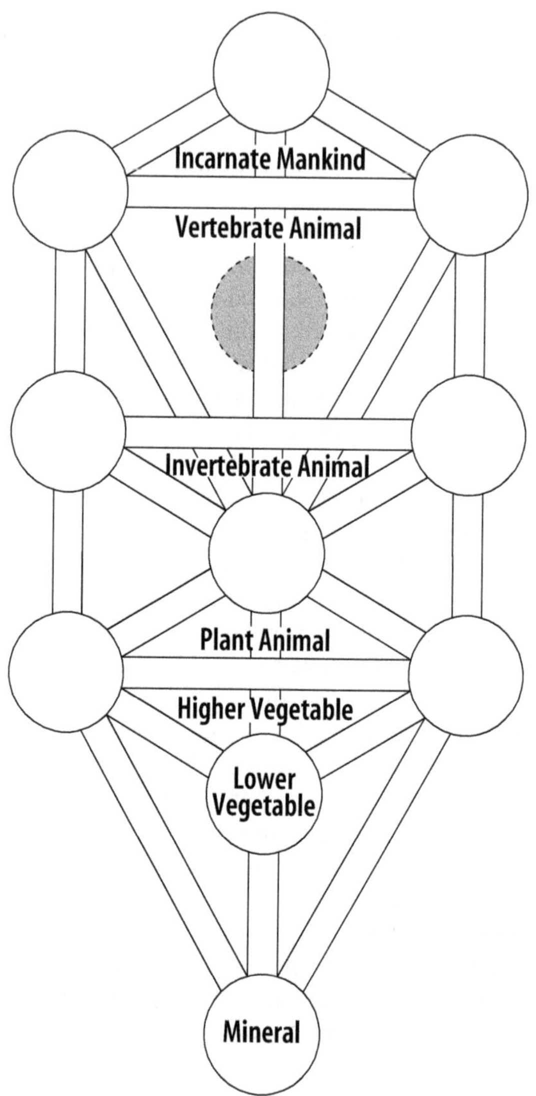

Figure 26—EVOLUTION

These are the seven levels of organic consciousness within terrestrial evolution. Every creature is a sensitive part of a vast matrix that participates in the general plan of Providence. Each zone increases the planet's consciousness by its experience. Thus, Nature can serve as an arena for trial and error in uplifting the level of the Solar system. (Halevi)

22. *Sequence*

Organic life on Earth is possible because the cosmic conditions within the Solar system are just right at this point in time. All life depends on the Sun while the Moon and the planets regulate the cycles of growth and development.

The mineral kingdom supports all organic life. The vegetable level of Nature varies from the most primitive organisms to delicate flowers or massive trees. The division between vegetable and animal kingdoms is not clear-cut as there are creatures which sometimes operate like plants and at other times behave like animals. The development of brains and nervous systems, however simple, marks out the invertebrates. They have possibilities quite different from plants as their capacity for interaction with their environment is much greater.

The level of vertebrate animals resonates with the lower part of Yezirah, indicating that these creatures may have an interior dimension. Anyone living with a cat or a dog can observe a degree of thought and feeling in their pets which even appear to have dreams.

Not so long ago in the timescale of the planet, the apes were the most advanced species on Earth. Their bodies have a versatility not seen in other animals. For example, their hands can hold sticks and stones and use them as tools. The first humans were incarnated into primate bodies. What we see today is a much refined version of these early ancestors but one can still observe the primate in oneself. However, human beings have the capability of psychological and spiritual development that is unique to our species.

What then is the driving force of Evolution? Genetic mutations and natural selection exist as ideas in the World of Creation while different forms manifest in the World of Asiyyah. The process of refinement and improvement continues, most of all in human consciousness which extends far beyond physicality.

Figure 27—ART

Cave paintings like these animals are rare records of the imagination and skill of early humanity preserved up to our time. Little is known about other prehistoric art forms like music, dance and poetry which were part of the oral tradition. (Prehistoric cave art)

23. Humanity

Archaeological evidence suggests that the human species originated in Africa well over a million years ago and slowly migrated to other continents. Although the early branches of the human family tree withered away, those souls reincarnated into more advanced societies. Modern humans, *homo sapiens*, are now the leading edge of evolution.

Intelligence, curiosity and imagination are characteristics of the human mind. The development of language made it possible for knowledge to be passed on. Later, writing emerged because there was a need to record what could not be easily remembered as societies grew more complex and hierarchical.

The advancement in technology and improvement of living conditions have resulted in rapid population growth over the last century. There are now more young souls incarnated who have to learn quickly in order to become part of a global civilisation. However, there are also more mature souls with their accumulated experience of many lifetimes.

A human being is a microcosm of Existence. All the levels of Jacob's Ladder are present in potential. The vast majority of people are still at the vegetable level of psychological development, their main interests being food and propagation. The animal level people are more awake in their ambition to gain power and status in society. The truly human individuals are not dominated by these instincts as they have a wider and deeper outlook.

While the planet Earth receives and processes celestial influences, humanity is its finest instrument in its ability to respond to cosmic cycles. Because human beings are the organs of perception for the Holy One, they can appreciate their environment in a way that no mineral, plant or animal has ever done.

Figure 28—INTERACTION

Organic life on Earth can exist from the bottom of the ocean to the lower atmosphere. This biosphere is full of interaction where every creature has a specific function. This hierarchy follows the metaphysical model of Jacob's Ladder but within a cellular framework. (19th century print)

24. *Life*

The principle of Life originates from the World of Emanation. Organic life on Earth is but an intermediary stage as entities come into and pass out of physical existence. Death and decay are part of the process whereby matter is being recycled.

Nature would not flourish without the assistance of nature spirits. They operate at the etheric or electromagnetic level of physicality. Folk traditions are full of stories about them as their presence can sometimes be discerned by sensitive people. These beings are said to have their own hierarchy within their elemental dimension and even human habitations.

People who have had a glimpse of the afterlife often describe it as being more alive than the earthly existence. The psyche is immortal, that is, it survives physical death and continues living in the Treasure House of Souls. Here in Paradise, without the constraints of the body, the full essence of the soul shines through.

It is not uncommon that, in a heightened state of consciousness, one may perceive the whole universe as a living and interconnected entity. Such a transpersonal vision is not always a subjective spiritual experience. It can be an objective insight into the realm of angels and archangels.

Deep within every human being is the eternal Divine spark which is witness to all that was, is and shall be.

Wheel Of Life And Death

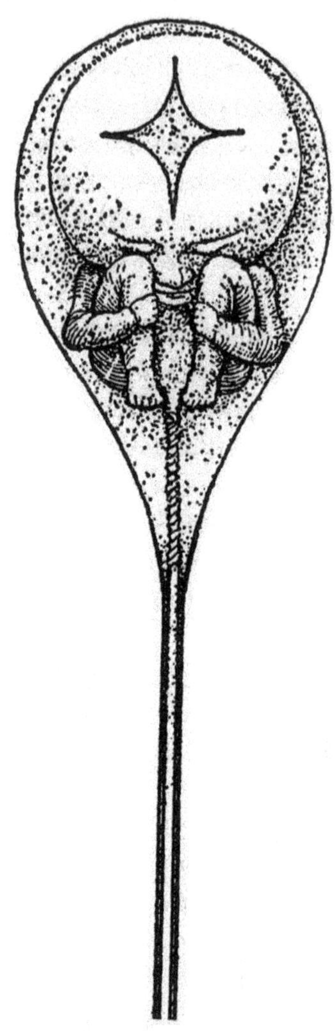

Figure 29—EMBRYO

At the moment of conception, the genetic inheritances of both parents fuse together. From this point on, the psyche begins to acquire an organic vehicle so that it can operate in the physical world. Later in life, the quality of the soul inhabiting the body will overlay and modify the family characteristics up to a point. (Hartsoeker, 17th century)

25. Gestation

When the egg of the mother is fertilised by the sperm of the father, it is the beginning of a new microcosmic universe. The young embryo undergoes the metamorphosis of Evolution from a single cell through plant and animal before it starts to develop a distinctly human form. This process is monitored by the laws of Nature as well as spiritual mentors.

Prior to incarnation, the soul resides in the Treasure House of Souls as long as necessary and perhaps meets old companions of the same soul group while preparing for the next life. Timing is crucial as the soul has to fit into a particular operation and generation.

Sometimes a couple making love becomes aware of the presence of the person about to be conceived. There is usually a karmic reason why a soul coming down to incarnation is allocated to particular parents. Initially the bond is tenuous but as the foetus grows in the womb, so the soul and the couple become increasingly attached to each other.

At this prenatal stage, the mother's wellbeing is vitally important. Any imbalance or extreme situation can be a source of a physical or psychological problem to emerge later in life. For example, a person may be affected by something that was actually the mother's experience.

The incoming soul's personal karma and level of awareness can also be part of the prenatal development. Some are reluctant to be born and may retard the process of gestation, while others are very happy to start a new incarnation. Sometimes just prior to birth, the outline of the future is shown so that the soul would recognise the crucial points of their fate later in life.

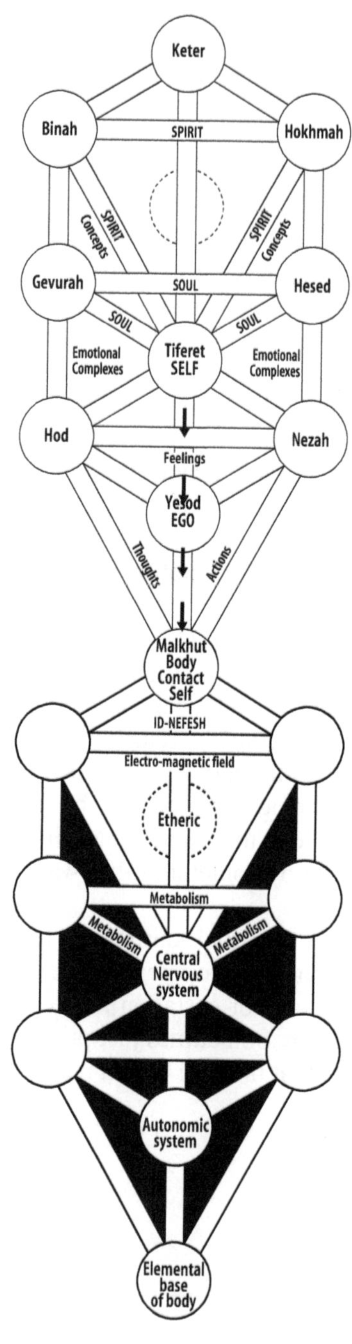
Keter
Binah
SPIRIT
Hokhmah
SPIRIT
Concepts
SPIRIT
Concepts
Gevurah
SOUL
Hesed
SOUL
SOUL
Emotional Complexes
Tiferet SELF
Emotional Complexes
Hod
Nezah
Feelings
Yesod EGO
Thoughts
Actions
Malkhut Body Contact Self
ID-NEFESH
Electro-magnetic field
Etheric
Metabolism
Metabolism
Metabolism
Central Nervous system
Autonomic system
Elemental base of body

26. Birth

When a baby arrives and takes its first breath, its own body clocks start ticking. The three biorhythms are all critical at the beginning as the baby encounters the world of the four elements and begins an independent life outside the mother. The first day can be a big shock.

It will take many years before the central nervous system is fully integrated with the psyche. While the newborn infant cannot speak, its eyes reveal an adult awareness. These initial seven days are called the first age of wisdom. Then, it is said, an angel tweaks the baby's nose and it forgets the memories of its previous existence as the demands of the body take over.

Besides the body clock, the moment of birth also sets the cosmic configuration of the person's horoscope in place as the fluidic mode of the psyche crystallises into a particular character which will fit into a fatal pattern. The time and place of birth are no accident but carefully chosen by Providence. This setup indicates both the karma of the past and the plan for the present life.

Although the newborn looks much like any other baby, one may be able to perceive what kind of person is going to emerge. This impression is called the *zelem* or etheric form which will slowly fill out in the process of growth, until it is fully manifest in the adult.

Figure 30—VEHICLES (Left)

Sometimes the body, psyche and the spirit are defined as different "vehicles". Here at the moment of birth, the psyche interlocks with the body. The incoming soul will have a personal fate and maybe a transpersonal destiny to fulfil. (Halevi)

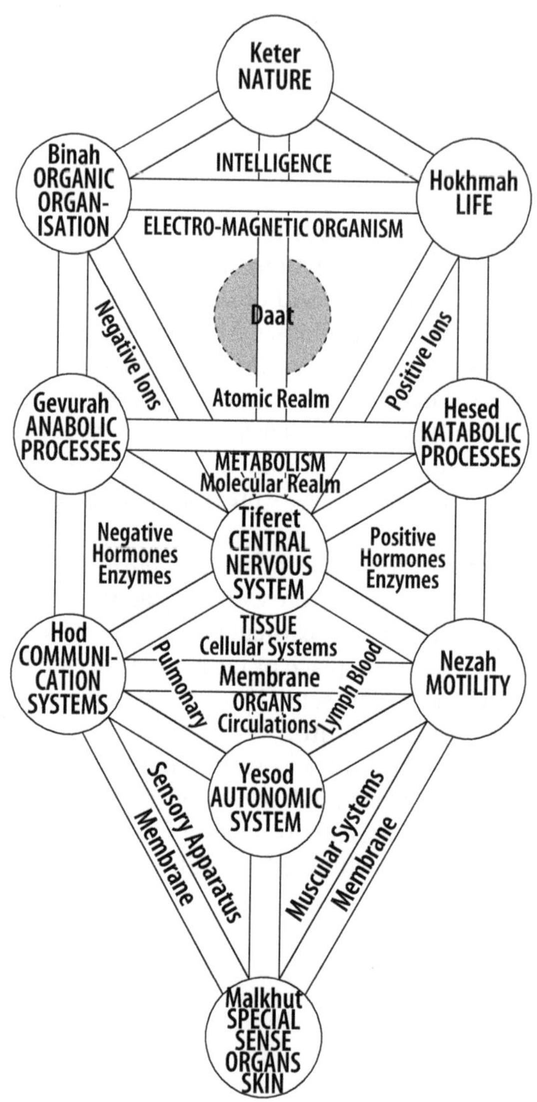

Figure 31—STRUCTURE

The universal model of the sefirotic Tree is manifest in the structure and dynamic of the body. Nature provides the instinctive intelligence of Evolution which is sometimes wiser than the psyche. When the life principle departs at death, the physical body begins to dissolve back into the four elements. (Halevi)

27. Body

Having started off as a single cell, the body grows until it reaches its full maturity. This organic machine never stops as millions of unseen processes keep it functional. However, over every seven years, almost all the cells in the body have been replaced with new ones, the form being contained in the etheric zelem so that the body looks more or less the same in spite of changes.

Many people identify with their body completely and believe that is all who they are. They are preoccupied with making their body attractive so as to get the best possible mate. That is part of the evolutionary process of Mother Nature. So too are the clothes which become part of one's body image. The garments are designed not only to protect from the elements but also to express one's status in society.

Most people are usually quite unaware of this process which dominates their lives. Their body language, however, might be obvious to an observer. Fear and anger or love and joyousness express themselves easily through the body. The posture of a top dog is very different from that of an underdog.

The path of interior development often begins with some physical discipline like yoga. The instinctive body is like a wild horse that needs to be trained. Once under conscious control, the body becomes a fine instrument by which one can act out one's purpose in life be it physical, psychological or spiritual. An advanced individual might even embody Divinity in their daily life.

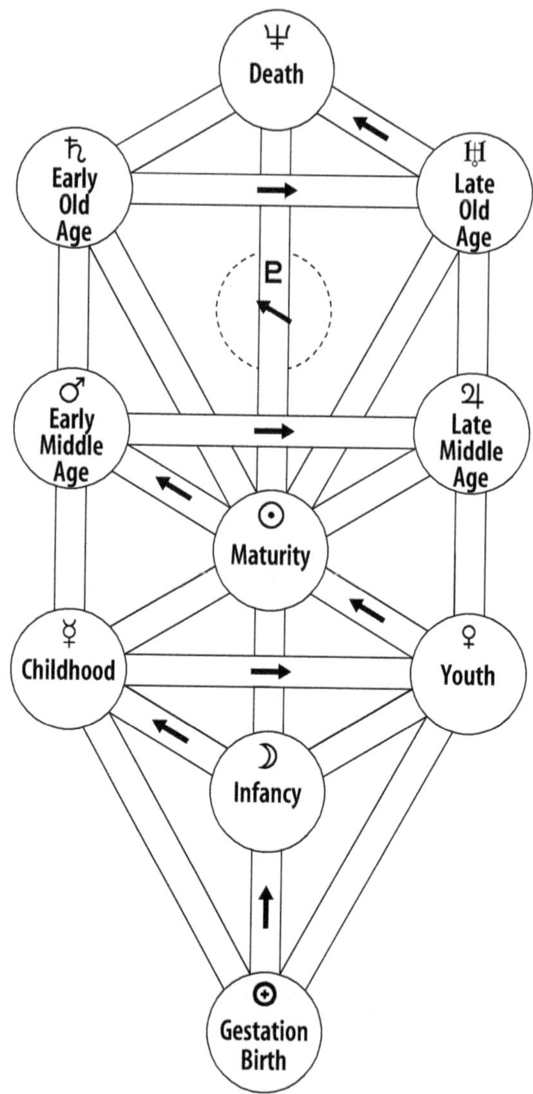

Figure 32—LIFETIME

Here we see the sefirotic Tree extended in time in the ascending Lightning Flash. A lifetime is considered to be composed of approximately seven year periods, each ruled by a particular planetary principle. In earlier generations, not many lived to a ripe old age. Now it is not uncommon to live beyond the Uranian period. Unfortunately the Neptunian age prior to death is sometimes lost in the fog of dementia when the brain, but not always the psyche, breaks down. (Halevi)

28. *Maturation*

The foundation of a particular incarnation is laid in the first seven years of infancy. That is a period when the ego is formed as the child learns to relate to its family and environment. Governed by the Moon/ Yesod, this is also a time of psychic experiences and imagination.

The period of school and formal education is governed by Mercury/ Hod with its fascination for games, information and learning skills. The transition to puberty is often confusing when the age of Venus/ Nezah wakes up instinctive desires and passions which can manifest as pure sensuality or the idealism of youth.

At the Solar/Tiferet period of maturity, the body is at its peak and one is expected to be an adult. Most people take on the responsibility of family while others wander around in the search for an ideal animus or anima. The moment of truth comes in a life crisis when one reconsiders whether one's ambitions are realistic or just youthful fantasies. The early middle age is a time of the focus and discipline of Mars/Gevurah. Later, Jupiter/Hesed brings an expansive phase of interior and exterior growth.

The age of Saturn/Binah is a time of reflection when one recognises fatal patterns and lessons for this incarnation, while the period of Uranus/Hokhmah can give transpersonal insights into one's destiny. Finally, the age of Neptune/Keter may bring peace and acceptance.

However, one's level of development does not always correspond to the physical age. At present, one may be an old soul in a young body or a middle-aged person who is still juvenile. The planetary ages are designed by Providence not only for biological but also for psychological and spiritual maturation.

Figure 33 – HOME

Human beings have adapted to living in a wide variety of circumstances on the planet. This is the home of a nomadic family in Lappland. It is more than a shelter against the harsh conditions of the arctic winter. A home also strengthens the emotional bond between individuals as they spend much time together within the boundary of its walls. (Drawing by G.Berndtson, 19th century)

29. *Malkhut*

While incarnate, people need a place to live. A home is an important part of their interaction with the physical world. There is an instinctive need to belong somewhere, because without roots one is insecure and vulnerable.

The early humans were primarily hunter-gatherers. They moved around but needed shelter to protect them from the elements and animals. They learnt to use whatever material was available to build homes. Some were fortunate to find caves which they decorated with wall paintings, no doubt using animal skins as carpets and stones and logs as furniture. Animals are not known to decorate their homes; it is a distinctly human preoccupation.

The invention of farming made permanent settlements possible. With it came not only co-operation but also competition with neighbours. There was the desire to keep up with the latest developments and do better than others in order to increase one's status in society. It is part of human evolutionary process.

A home is also an expression of one's individuality with momentous objects of both personal and family history. Over time, people's sense of home expands to include their home town or home country. Those who move to faraway places may seek to recreate the old circumstances or they adjust to a new culture and develop a more global view.

While human beings have lived on Earth, their habitations have left their mark on the landscape, for better or worse. As more and more people gravitate towards cities, they may lose touch with their natural environment. However, their true home is not on this planet but in the higher Worlds.

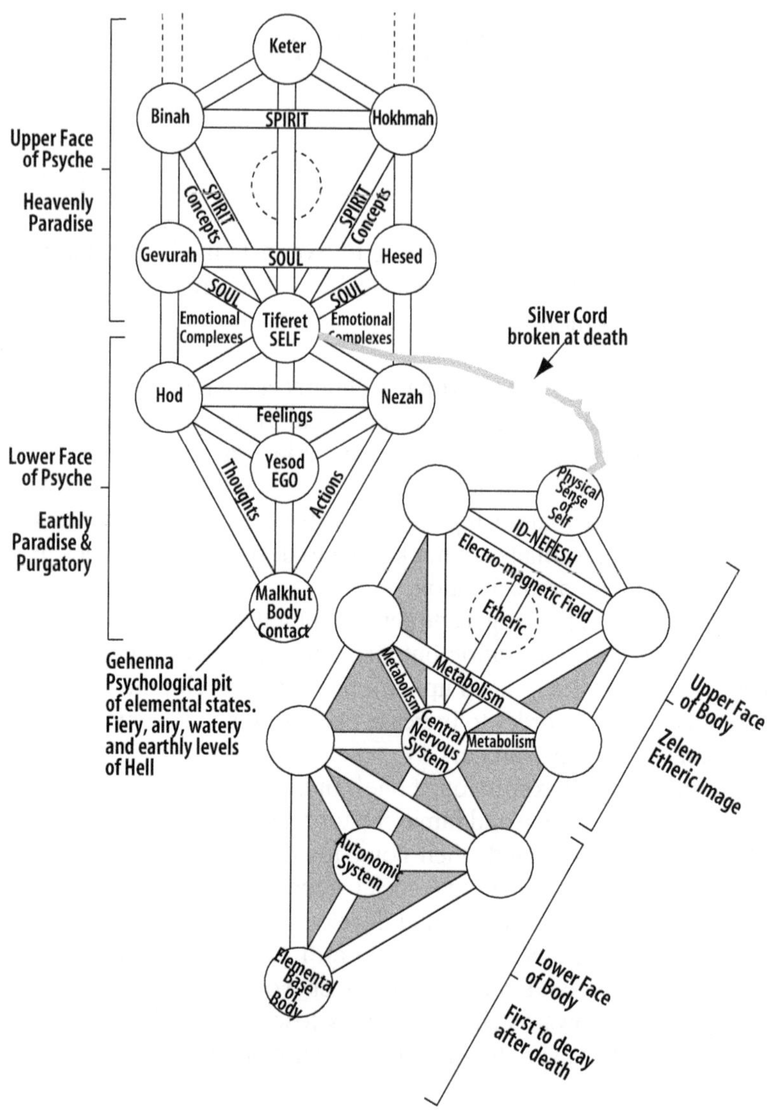

Figure 34—DISCONNECTION

The breaking of the silver cord is a symbolic way of describing the moment of death when the psyche is disconnected from the organic life of the body. However, the psyche does not die but continues to exist intact with all its memories, experience and consciousness, whereas the body begins to disintegrate back to the physical elements. (Halevi)

30. Death

Like birth, death is a transition from one World to another. There may be people around to wish you farewell but they cannot follow you to where you are going. Likewise there may be somebody waiting for you on the other side but ultimately you have to cross the border on your own.

Much of what is known about life after death comes from individuals who have been clinically dead but have been resuscitated. Often their first experience is to see a playback of their entire lifetime. There may be also a rising up through a dark tunnel, into a zone of light and a meeting either of family members or what appear to be wise guides. However, others report going downwards and seeing a glimpse of a very unpleasant place.

Death can happen at any age. The decease of a child or a young person is considered tragic whereas the elderly passing away is usually accepted as a normal process. The length of a lifetime may be preset at birth but it can be disrupted by wars or natural disasters when people come under the law of collective karma. However, some individuals are saved from such disasters by providential intervention which is regarded as miraculous.

Many people do not believe in the possibility of life after death, for whatever reason. There is a saying about an atheist's funeral: "All dressed up but nowhere to go." Those who contemplate the afterlife while still incarnate have an easier passage after their last breath.

In ancient times, it was the custom to bury the deceased with gifts and utensils for the afterlife. The funeral rites of different cultures have much in common. They are not only expressing personal bereavement and collective mourning but they are an acknowledgement of the uniqueness of each human life.

Figure 35—IMMORTALITY

Different religions and folklore describe the afterlife as a hierarchy of Hell, Purgatory, Paradise and Heaven. Vivid images of torment in Hell are meant to warn people about the consequences of their evil deeds while Purgatory gives the possibility of redemption. The very pleasant afterlife in Paradise is the most common destination while the pure and pious souls expect to reach one of the seven Heavens. (Egyptian Papyrus)

31. Afterlife

Immediately after death, the psyche is still able to connect with the physical World for a few days, until the etheric vehicle is dispersed. That is when apparitions are sometimes seen as the deceased come to say goodbye to their loved ones. According to many esoteric traditions, an individual then enters a period of deep reflection when the reality of the life left behind becomes obvious as one can not hide from the truth. This can be painful in what is called a state of Purgatory but vital for the soul's development and future lives.

If the person turns away from the path of honesty, their denial draws them down. The seven levels of Hell are usually described in terms of harsh elemental conditions like being burnt, frozen or buried in mud. This graded series of punishments is designed to awaken the conscience. Some souls avoid going through the postmortem process and become earthbound ghosts that haunt certain places, maybe for centuries.

Those who acknowledge their mistakes and endure remorse rise into the domain of Paradise. What some traditions call the Summerlands can resemble a beautified version of a familiar place on Earth. Here one can spend a pleasant time with discarnate friends and relatives.

Those who have consciously developed their soul rise to the upper Paradise. There they gravitate towards their particular field of interest and maybe even meet their particular soul group. The most advanced individuals will go on to the Heavenly Halls where they meet their spiritual peers in the "Academies on High".

One lifetime is not enough. There is always unfinished business, karmic debts to be paid and more to be learnt. The latter period of the afterlife is a preparation for the next incarnation with its fate and destiny.

History

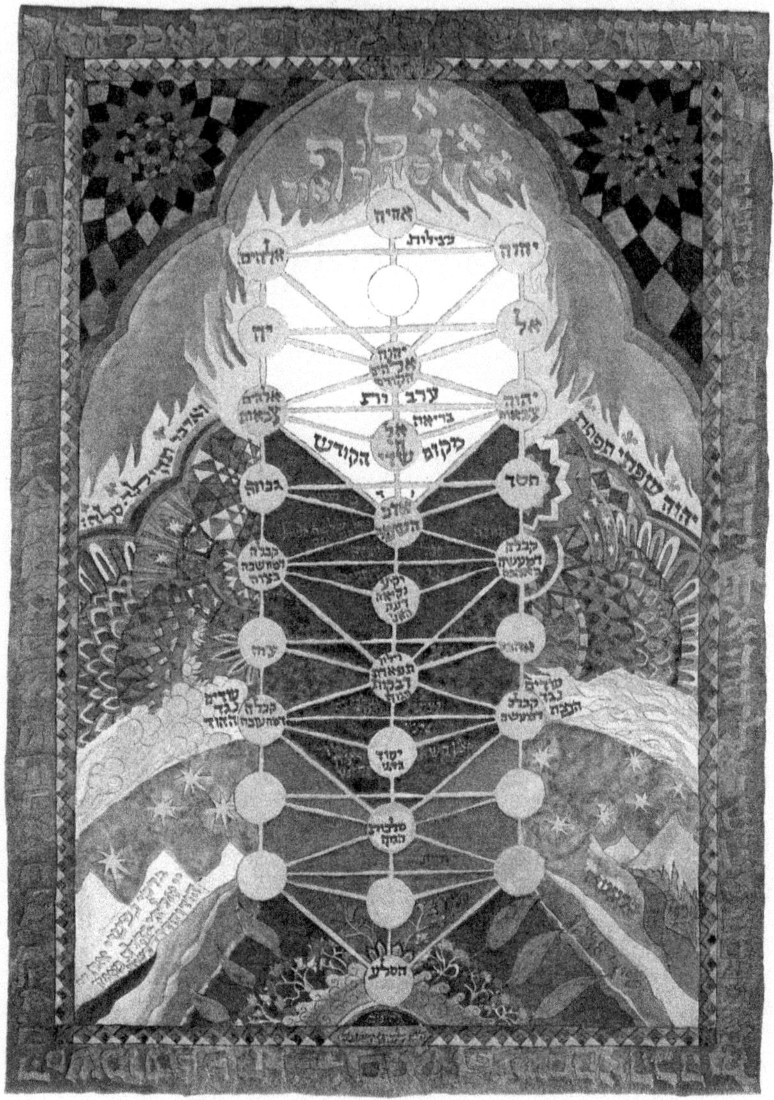

Figure 36—PARGOD

According to early kabbalistic literature, there is a great Cosmic Curtain or 'Pargod' hanging before the Throne of Heaven setting out the patterns of history. Each thread in its weave represents a person's path through many lives. Gold threads symbolise the most advanced individuals, whom the ancient Greeks called heroes, while the silver and copper stand for uncommon and common people. In Kabbalah they are called the human, animal and vegetable levels of humanity. (Painting by Prof. James Russell, 20th century)

32. Four Journeys

The journey of humanity began in the higher Worlds. Each individual started as pure consciousness in the World of Azilut before acquiring a spirit in the World of Creation and a psyche in the World of Formation. Humans resided in this Treasure House of Souls until they incarnated into the World of Action. This sequence is called the First Journey.

It is said that at our present point in history most people have already made their First Journey and they are now living a series of fates on their Second Journey. Beginning as young souls, they slowly learnt how to live on earth in simple tribal circumstances. This epoch usually leaves a strong impression on the soul. This is why a particular culture or area may always feel like 'home'.

The Third Journey is that of destiny. It begins with a spiritual awakening when one shifts from just a personal fate into perceiving a cosmic purpose of Existence. Where such a momentous event took place is dimly remembered as one's 'spiritual home country'. It takes many lifetimes' training as an apprentice and a journeyman before one is a master and one's destiny becomes operational. Thus the two journeys run parallel over many lives.

The most advanced individuals on this third stage become crucial people of destiny. They may be great teachers, scholars or even statesmen who know what their mission is. They are less bound to the Wheel of Life and Death but they volunteer to come down to help humanity.

The Fourth Journey will be that of Resurrection at the End of Time when the great Curtain of Existence is rolled up. According to Tradition, then every person has to account for their overall performance before returning to their original position within the radiance of Adam Kadmon.

Figure 37—ARK

The story of Noah's ark can be seen as a metaphor of a school of the soul. Facing an imminent disaster, Noah and his family preserved knowledge, symbolised by the living animals, so that civilisation could start again after the Flood. Humanity has encountered similar dark events since then. However, the schools have taken precautions to preserve what was good so that previous achievements were not lost. (Rev. T.Bankes's Bible, 19th century)

33. Legends

Apart from geological and archaeological evidence, much esoteric knowledge of the prehistoric period is buried in ancient legends. By the time these stories were written down, however, much had been embroidered by primitive imagination, political propaganda and distortion. One needs to be open-minded and discriminating in order to find the archetypal and metaphysical principles behind myths, legends and sacred structures.

Taken literally, the biblical legend of Noah and the Flood could be referring to an actual event. The story of a flood is quite common throughout the Middle East.

Allegorically, the morality of the story is the consequences of evil. In this case, the evil generation was destroyed by Divine intervention in the form of the Flood. More often evil destroys itself by corruption and violence.

One can observe the metaphysical aspect in the structure of the Ark. In its three decks and a cubit above, it resembles the fourfold layout of Solomon's Temple with its outer court, inner court, sanctuary and the Holy of Holies. The male and female animals of each species represent the active and passive principles of life, including Noah and his three sons with their wives. Likewise, the seven pairs of animals may be seen as the sevenfold levels of organic consciousness while the forty days and nights at sea indicate a complete cycle of a supernatural event.

The mystical aspect of this legend can be experienced in the manifestation of Divine Light in the form of a rainbow with its seven colours after the Flood. Such an insight can be awesome.

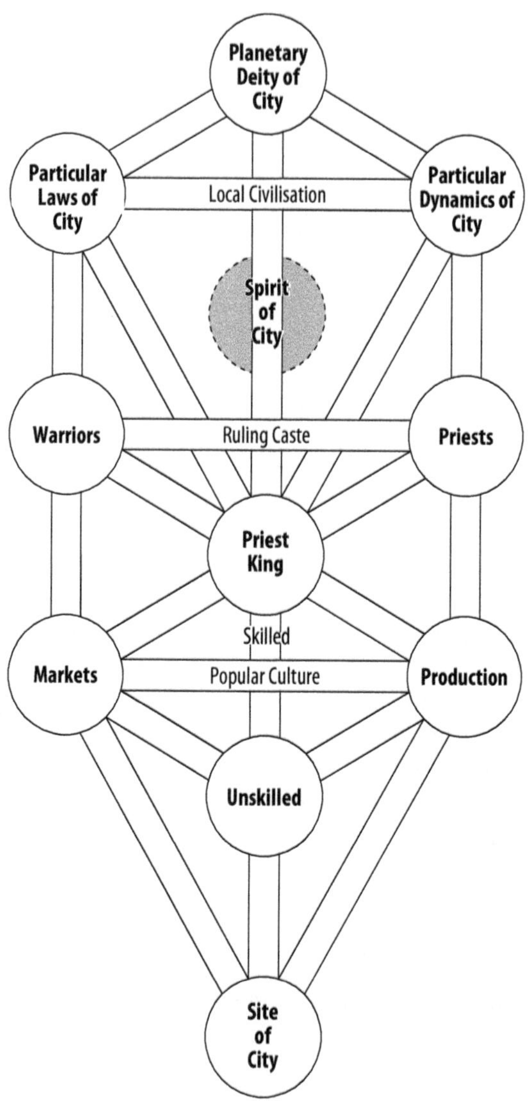

Figure 38—HIERARCHY
Cities have different functions depending on their locality. Cities often evolved on the site of ancient trading posts and market towns but some were deliberately founded either as commercial centres or to glorify a particular ruler. The stratification of the population usually settled according to the archetypal principles of the sefirotic Tree. (Halevi)

34. City

A purely tribal way of life has a strict code of conduct which locks people in their respective roles and allows little space for individuality. When cities started to emerge in the ancient world, they naturally attracted the most talented and enterprising from the surrounding area as cities offered more opportunities than the routine of rural life. Cities are like alchemical retorts in that they transform people who want to develop.

The evolution of trade and industry in cities gave rise to specialist artisan and merchant classes. Trade routes spread out to connect with other cultures. As the cities grew more wealthy, they could afford to support arts and universities, often encouraged by their rulers.

The fortunes of an early city depended on the calibre of its ruler. Ideally the ruler was both a religious and political leader but many were seduced by power and led their city-states to competitive and disastrous wars. Sometimes it was the priests who were the real power behind the throne as advisors to the king. The priestly authority was also important in formulating and implementing laws which are the basis of any civilised society.

A city depends on natural resources like water and fertile land. Many once-prosperous cities are now but ruins in a desert as the climate changed after the ice age. However, the field force created by city life can still be perceived at some sites. Such an atmosphere is an amalgam of the city's history, function and all the people who lived there.

Ancient city-states were an important transition from barbarity towards nationhood and civilisation. Some cities had a particular destiny to become cultural and political capitals. Such cosmopolitan entities are still the focus and cutting edge of human development.

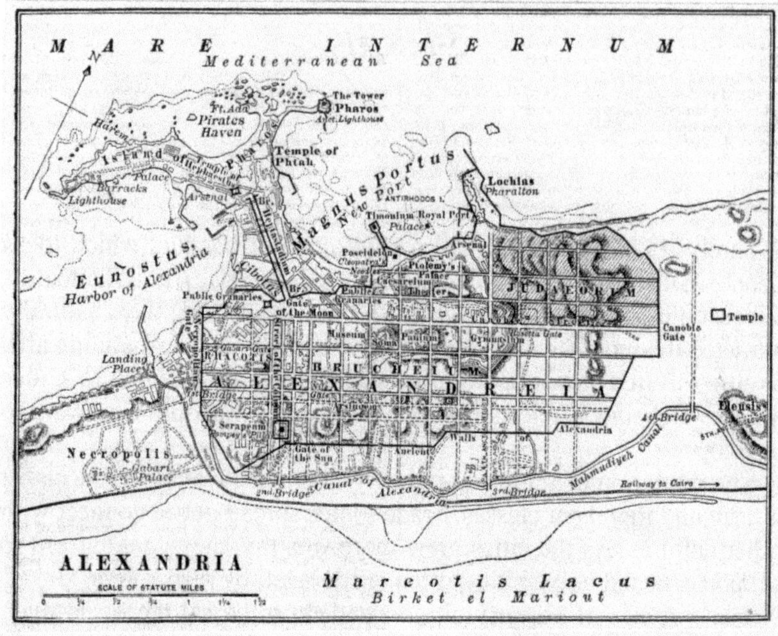

Figure 39—CENTRE

Alexandria in Egypt was the cosmopolitan capital of the eastern Mediterranean for centuries. It had communities from all over the Middle East and connections with Africa, Asia and Europe. The museum, with its university and library, had a particular significance as the centre of learning and new developments like Neoplatonism, which later had a profound effect on Western schools of the soul.
(Map of ancient Alexandria, Jewish Encyclopaedia)

35. Capital

A capital city is the Tiferet of a nation. As such, it has a particular role in all areas of development. Its streets, buildings and monuments have witnessed the continuity of history, providing a setting for individual and collective activities as generations of souls have passed through it.

One characteristic of a capital is cosmopolitanism. Foreign commerce is focused there attracting traders from far beyond the nation's borders. For example, Peter the Great first encountered European culture visiting the German colony in Moscow which subsequently led to the modernisation of medieval Russia. Foreign embassies and diplomats naturally set up their residences in the capital even in most remote countries.

Besides government and trade, a capital city is the centre of many other activities from education to entertainment. There is often fierce competition between talented people creating a need for excellence in every field. The availability of museums, libraries and cultural events shifts the level of sophistication of the general population.

Many spiritual and humanitarian movements started in capital cities which are still the home of their headquarters, from Masonic temples to charitable institutions. Behind the scenes are to be found schools of the soul which operate discreetly but nevertheless have a profound effect on the society.

Sometimes a particular soul group incarnates on a special mission to start a new impulse in human development. For a brief period in history, a city may become the spiritual capital where the most advanced individuals come to work together. Such brilliant epochs have taken place, for example, in ancient Athens and medieval Baghdad. In the Judeo-Christian tradition, the ultimate spiritual capital is the indestructible archetype of the Heavenly Jerusalem.

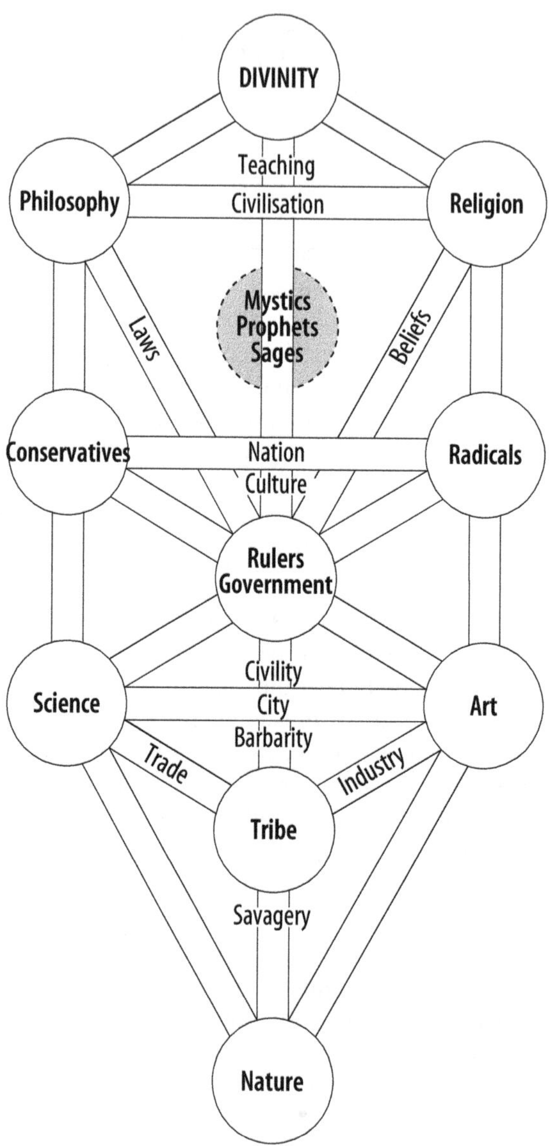

Figure 40—SOCIETY

A society is the progression of human Evolution and a composition of widely diverse elements. It is the task of the government as the Tiferet of the nation to keep the society in balance. Even so, there is a natural oscillation between the left and right pillars according to the mood of the time. (Halevi)

36. Civilisation

While savage and barbaric communities have their identity in their tribal culture, civilisation begins with cities. In a city, people from different origins have to learn to live together and to find a common identity. In order to manage and organise a large number of people, a city needs a government and a civil service. This can be an embryo of a nation.

Nationhood evolves slowly and it usually needs a strong leader to unite villages, towns and cities into an alliance, either by force or by skilful diplomacy. A nation is an entity with a particular sense of identity based on its location and history. Some countries have distinct boundaries defined by sea or mountains while elsewhere national borders may have changed many times in the course of history.

In some cases, development may come with the advent of empires that are often just temporary political structures. Even Rome disintegrated but the idea of common laws, currency and safe travel as well as a wide cultural interaction left a model copied by others later. So it was that subject peoples often adopted the ways of their conquerors. Out of this came an improved way of life that created opportunities not seen in the barbaric epoch.

The concept of civilisation is based on deeper values than power politics. Western civilisation is rooted in the Ten Commandments as well as the Greek and Roman political system. While religion gives the basic rules for a just society, it needs mystics, prophets and sages in every generation to refresh and renew the message. Otherwise a civilisation can crystallise and degenerate.

Even civilised nations can regress to tribal savagery as seen in the two World Wars. Since then, the United Nations is a manifestation of an emerging global civilisation. Trade routes are now worldwide and new ideas and inventions spread rapidly through international networks.

Religion

Figure 41—CREATION
Religion is concerned with the relationship between God, humanity and the universe. An example is the biblical story of Creation in Genesis that explains the Divine origin of Existence. In this, God is outside time and space but the Creator can intervene in the universe and even communicate with human beings. More often it is humans who speak to God in the form of prayers. (Lucas Cranach. 16th century print)

37. Faith

Faith is usually a blend of an individual's trust in their personal interior experience and a traditional belief system passed on through generations. Prehistoric man realised quite early on that a human being is not all powerful and there were invisible supernatural forces that influenced mundane affairs. Such belief gave rise to various Nature and Sky gods.

Such entities needed to be placated and worshipped in hope that they would grant whatever was needed for a good life. Human and animal sacrifices were not uncommon amongst savage and barbaric tribes. As not everybody wished to approach the gods themselves, shamans and priests arose as intermediaries.

With the rise of formal religion people were taught about a code of conduct. What was needed to please God was the fulfilling of the commandments. For most people that was enough as they felt secure in the customs and traditions of their religion.

However, the quality of real faith is deeply emotional as it is a matter of an individual's soul level. It may include both fear of God at Gevurah and love of God at Hesed or just a quiet certainty of being in the presence of the Holy One at Tiferet. Such faith has the power to sustain a person even in most difficult circumstances.

If one is sincere in one's faith, one may be granted a genuine mystical experience. It may come through one's own effort in prayer and meditation or as an act of Grace. It may come in the form of a vision, hearing an interior voice or perceiving the touch of the Holy Spirit. Such an experience becomes deeply ingrained in the soul and is not easily forgotten.

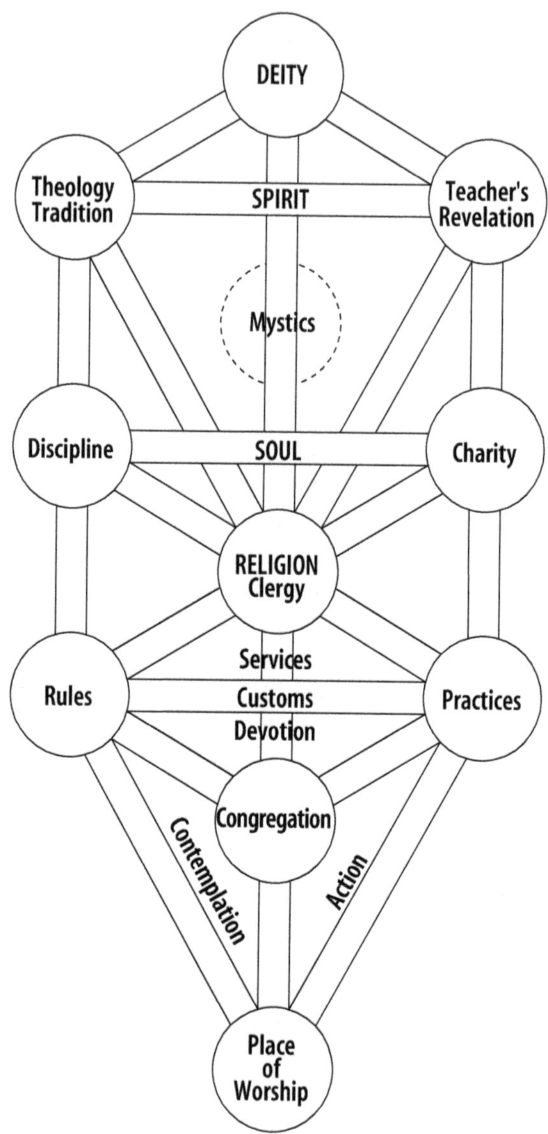

Figure 42—ESTABLISHMENT

A religion begins usually with a small number of people who support a Master. The Teacher's revelation may be quite a different insight into spirituality, so as to meet the need of the time, or a reformation of the existing Tradition. Either way, the belief must conform to cosmic principles or it will never take root as a grounded tradition. (Halevi)

38. Tradition

The Age of Pisces from c.500 BCE to c.1600 CE was to be one of Religion. Most of the major Traditions were formulated by the Middle Ages. Since the Age of Reason began c.1600, at least in the West, the social and political power of the religious establishment began to diminish while non-conformist belief systems started to flourish.

There is usually an inspired Teacher at the beginning of a new spiritual movement. Such a seminal period can last for two or three generations. If there are enough committed people to organise the movement, it may become a Tradition that lasts for decades or centuries.

Although the original inspiration may be quite simple, over time it becomes embroidered into a vast theology. A written tradition is necessary as it gives a common framework for all followers. However, books alone can not keep a Tradition alive, it needs to be practised. That puts a big responsibility on those who are the leaders.

Therefore, the role of the clergy is crucial. The priests safeguard the continuity of the Tradition as well as being there to perform ceremonies, teach and inspire the congregation. Alas, when power and money are involved, the wrong kind of people can be attracted to the priesthood. The Tradition may then crystallise into an orthodoxy or, worse, start forcefully converting or persecuting non-believers.

On the positive side, spiritual movements can have an uplifting influence. The principles of discipline and charity in particular are a training ground for the soul. Much sacred art and music has been produced to create a receptive atmosphere in the meeting place and to remind people of the Glory of God.

Figure 43—RITUAL
On a Day of Atonement, the Jewish community fasts and prays to be written into the Book of Life for the next year. It is a long day full of communal ceremonies and private supplications that require great physical as well as much internal effort, as seen in the stress of the congregation. This exercise involves the body, soul and spirit. (Yom Kippur service. 18th century print)

39. Way of Action

The purpose of a ritual is to inform the body that something out of the ordinary is taking place. The conscious alignment of the body and the mind reinforces the intention of the exercise. Rituals can be performed in solitude or collectively and they can be traditional or freshly created. What matters most is focused attention, otherwise the ritual can become meaningless routine.

The most obvious Way of Action can be observed in religious ceremonies. Sometimes the congregation is asked to participate by standing up, kneeling or prostrating. Often a subtle gesture like bowing one's head or joining hands is enough to reinforce an interior and spiritual intention.

Most established rituals follow a daily, weekly or annual cycle. Food plays an important part from fasting to feasting. Sharing bread and wine as well as lighting candles is a common custom. Some traditions have elaborate rituals to evoke a sacred mood.

Motivation is crucial. For example, a symbolic gesture can be used to express remorse. In medieval times this sometimes took a painful form in self-flagellation. In contrast the Sufi mode of spinning while they circled around each other shifted them up to cosmic cycles and beyond.

A pilgrimage is a Way of Action that has been practised since ancient times. A pilgrim is not just a tourist but someone who visits a sacred site with a spiritual aim in mind. To touch the Wailing Wall of the Temple often shifts individuals into another dimension. Ideally, one's whole life can be acted out like a pilgrimage.

Figure 44—STUDY

This room of Benedict de Spinoza, the philosopher, bears witness to a contemplative life. The house, now a museum, still has a highly charged atmosphere of profound thought and solemn quietude as well as intense concentration. It was here that he combined ancient, medieval and contemporary metaphysics with medieval Kabbalah. This had great appeal to an open-minded intelligentsia that sought to perceive reality beyond just Faith. (19th century print)

40. Way of Contemplation

The usual mode of the intellect is passive, that is, using conclusions based upon accepted information. The art of contemplation is to make the mind active by asking questions. Not only 'What?' but also 'Why?', 'Who?' and 'Where?' are useful tools leading to unexpected insights behind the obvious.

One can address the question to one's own unconscious or to one's inner teacher. Some use the technique of opening the Bible at random or casting the coins of the I Ching to show a way forward. The aim of contemplation is to improve one's own understanding and to present one's conclusions to others.

A contemplative group of companions is very helpful. Here interaction sparks off perhaps a new train of thought. Writing also helps to clarify vague concepts. It is said that the best way to learn is to teach. However, this requires acute conscious attention. Otherwise "the notes of a teacher become the notes of a student without passing through the mind of either".

By using the Tree of Life and Jacob's Ladder, a kabbalist can gain a detailed comprehension of a topic as well as its different levels. To find a solution to a problem usually requires looking at it either from above or from below. Once the basic principles are in focus, the higher intellect of Binah and Hokhmah will activate the unconscious and the process can become both methodical and inspirational.

The discipline of contemplation can be part of one's religious practice as it is said that God enjoys good conversation. While pondering the mysteries of Existence, one can address the questions directly to the Holy One.

Figure 45—FOCUS
Light is a symbol of the Divine. It is common to many mystical traditions to have some sort of illumination to hold the attention. It may be a simple candle, a stained glass window or an interior point of light. Such a focus may open up the higher centres of the brain or imagination that gives an impression or even a vision of the Divine Realm. (Drawing by Halevi)

41. Way of Devotion

Devotion is very much an interior practice, the way of the heart. For some it comes naturally, others have to learn it. The art is to retreat within oneself. Sitting still with eyes closed is one method to turn away from external impressions but we can hold the devotional frame of mind even in the midst of everyday life if we practise.

However, the interior world can also be distracting with its wandering thoughts and feelings. There are several modes for calming the mind. One is focusing the attention by repeating a Holy Name or a prayer. The aim here is to lift consciousness up from the mundane to the feeling triad and from there higher towards Tiferet and beyond.

Devotion offers many opportunities to shift levels because of its emotional power. Parts of religious services are especially designed to create a pious atmosphere which can transform the mood of the congregation. One needs to make an internal effort to be receptive, otherwise familiar hymns and prayers can pass without much effect. Even in private practice, one method may wear out and one needs to find a fresh approach.

An act of devotion invokes love which, ideally, touches one's Hesed. This can be directed towards a particular spiritual master so that one may experience a reflection of the admired qualities. When love is directed towards the Holy One, the devotee can enter the radiant presence of the Divine.

Having experienced such higher states of being, it may be difficult to accept coming back into the everyday world. In extreme cases, some speak about the dark night of the soul when they endure a dull, dry or otherwise uncomfortable period. Therefore devotion should always be grounded and supported by the ways of action and contemplation.

Figure 46—JACOB'S DREAM

Jacob had to leave his parents' home and face an uncertain future. While he stayed overnight in the wilderness, he had an extraodinary dream. He saw a ladder reaching from Earth to Heaven with angels ascending and descending. From above, God spoke to him. The ladder is an archetypal symbol of different levels of Existence while the "messengers" indicate a chain of communication between the lowest and the highest. (18th century print)

42. Prophecy

Dreams, visions and prophecy give insights into the higher Worlds. The Bible has many examples, as does kabbalistic literature. One of the most potent is the prophet Elijah, a manifestation of Enoch, who is said to be the Teacher of teachers. He appears to instruct or protect people who are worthy of such intervention.

Prophetic dreams can come in a symbolic form. An example is the Pharaoh's dream about seven fat and seven thin cows which Joseph was able to interpret as indicating seven years of abundance and seven years of famine and that appropriate action should be taken. Yet he did not claim the gift for himself but acknowledged that the answers were given by God.

A prophet's vision can have far-reaching consequences. Ezekiel's vision of the celestial Chariot inspired the *Merkabah* tradition. However, what is generally understood by prophecy is the ability to predict future events. Some prophets have been remarkably accurate while others have failed.

Kabbalah makes a distinction between greater and lesser prophets. The Bible warns against so called false prophets. These may be charismatic people with some psychic ability who deliberately set out to deceive the gullible or they may sincerely believe what they see and manage to convince others. It is usually only in hindsight that the truth is revealed. We have already passed several predicted deadlines for the end of the world.

When one stands on a high mountain top on a clear day, one sees a vast panorama in every direction. On a cloudy day, however, the visibility from the same place can be zero. The same may happen with interior vision. The clear air represents spiritual insight which can be obscured by one's psychological state. It takes much practice to learn discrimination.

Figure 47—MIRACLE

A miracle is a supernatural event when the higher Worlds seem to override the laws of Nature. Moses was the instrument of many miracles as he carried out what God had instructed him to do. His rod was the symbol of the staff of knowledge. When he struck the rock with it, water flowed out and saved the lives of the Israelites in the desert. Water symbolises nourishment of the soul. (Rev. T.Bankes's Bible, 19th century)

43. Exodus

The story of Exodus is commemorated every year in the Passover ceremony. Then everyone present is obliged to say, "When I was a slave in Egypt". When one participates in the Exodus personally, the story represents an individual's journey from physical and psychological slavery to spiritual freedom.

Slavery is an allegory of conditioning to habits and attitudes that keep a person in bondage to the everyday world. Like the Israelites, we are all bound by the conditioning that is necessary to exist in early life. This can prevent an individual from developing beyond tribal or social customs. It often takes a crisis to make people see their actual situation and wake them up.

For a journey, one needs a guide. The archetypal role of Moses as a teacher can come in the form of a wise friend. Sometimes a book that describes the possibility of another way of life can inspire the search for a school of the soul. In slavery, days and years go by in repetitive cycles. Crossing the Red Sea marks a point of no return when one is committed to an inner Exodus.

Going to the Promised Land is a strong incentive to continue the journey. However, the forty years in the desert represent a period of testing one's commitment. In this everyday life situation, one may be tempted to turn back into the security of slavery. One has to struggle against one's instinctive soul and subpersonalities that resist change. Some habits will not die off easily as the process of integration and individuation is opposed each day by our particular tribal and social patterns.

A Greek saying sums up the dilemma. "The secret of happiness is freedom. The secret of freedom is courage. That is why so many people fear happiness."

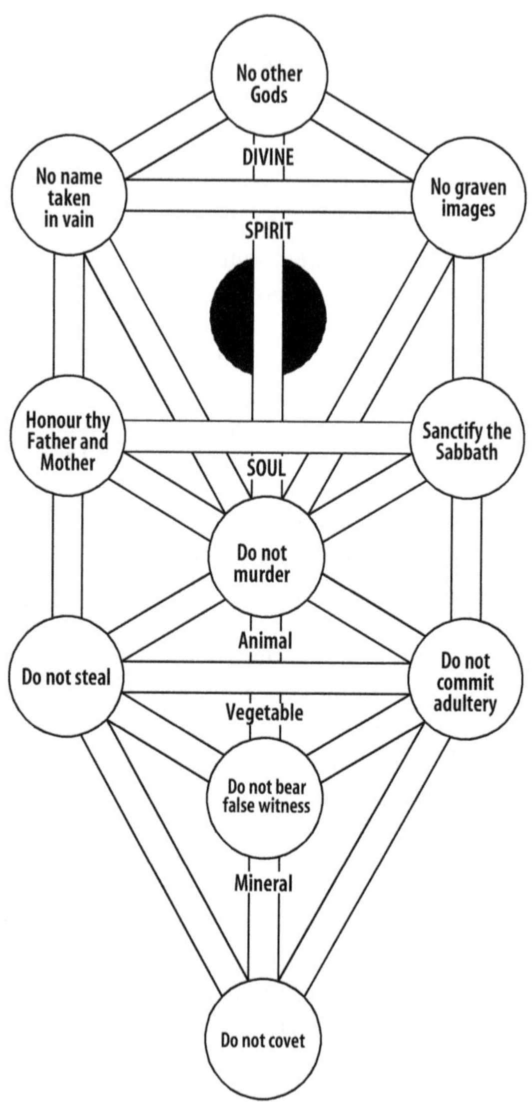

Figure 48—COMMANDMENTS

The ten commandments given to Moses were not only the basis of a civilised society but a spiritual discipline. The first three at the top are concerned with one's relationship with God and spirituality, while the middle three are for the benefit of the soul. The next three are to do with everyday life and social conduct. Finally, "Do not covet" at Malkhut refers to a root cause of many other transgressions. (Halevi)

44. Laws

The laws of Existence are based upon the ten principles of the sefirotic Tree. The variable factor is humanity with its free will. In this case human beings have been given a special set of laws. Here they have the choice between good and evil that no other celestial or terrestrial creature has.

The ten commandments can be seen as recommendations for how to conduct one's life. If one breaks any of these rules, there are inevitable consequences. For example, "coveting" may seem quite harmless but it can become an obsession that upsets the balance of the psyche, even leading to madness.

The commandments about false witness, stealing, adultery and murder are so fundamental to a just society that they are included in secular and criminal laws. However, these rules have also more subtle implications. For example, "false witness" can mean lying to oneself and blocking one's path of honesty, or one can "murder" one's own or another person's self-confidence.

The commandment of keeping the Sabbath is repeated several times in the Bible. This indicates its prime importance as sanctifying the day of rest refreshes the body, soul and spirit. "No other gods" at Keter is a warning not to obscure one's connection with the Divine source of life.

Other laws in the Bible such as "measure for measure" refer to the law of karma. Every action has a reaction. The sins of the fathers being visited upon their descendants means that there is also a collective karma which, in some cases, can expand to a historic karma of a nation.

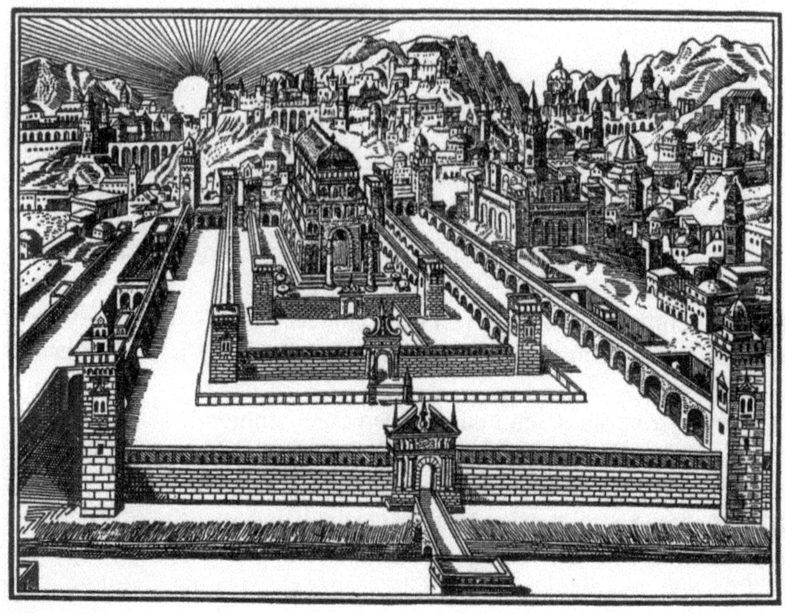

Figure 49—TEMPLE

Although this image is an idealised version of Solomon's Temple, its layout and structure are based upon archetypal principles. The outer court relates to the physical World, the inner court to the soul level and the sanctuary to the Spirit. The Holy of Holies represents the abode of Divinity within the three lower Worlds. (17th century print)

45. Worship

Moses was given detailed instructions for making the Tabernacle that was to be a moveable sanctuary for the Israelites in the desert. Later, Solomon's Temple was a more elaborate version and permanent place of worship. Most cultures built their temples to be a focus for their religious and national identity. Such sacred buildings are usually very conspicuous, rising high above all secular structures.

Religious worship is a formalised mode of devotion. It usually consists of prayers, sermons, music and rituals designed to invoke an awareness of the Divine. Although the service is the same for everybody in the congregation, the response can be very different depending on the level of people's development. Sometimes truly devout members of a congregation are more awake than the priest.

Most people are at the vegetable or animal levels. Their souls are as yet unawakened and their main concern is everyday life. For them the exoteric aspect of worship is sufficient as for the masses religion is primarily a tribal or national custom. They need the priests as intermediaries and parental archetypes.

The mesoteric or middle dimension consists of people at the human level who are in touch with their Tiferet. They are looking for a deeper meaning behind words and symbols as they want to know and understand for themselves. Numerous volumes of religious commentaries are written for them, not only as food for thought but as food for the soul.

The esoteric aspect of worship is a direct mystical experience of the Divine presence. The most beloved Psalm of David "The Lord is my shepherd" echoes such an experience. It gives the worshipper an inner certainty that is not erased by external circumstances.

Figure 50—MESSIAH
Moses was the Anointed of his time. He was able to communicate directly with God and stay in the Divine presence for a prolonged period. When he came down from Mount Sinai, his face was so radiant that people were afraid of him. From then on, he put a veil on his face when he was with people but he took it off when he spoke with God. (Rev. T. Bankes's Bible, 19th century)

46. Hierarchy

Human society is a hierarchy. This is seen in the structure of government, army and religious establishments. There is also an unseen spiritual hierarchy where the ranks are filled by people of destiny. These are old souls who incarnate in order to carry out a specific mission.

Some esoteric traditions speak about a Great Holy Council. These are the most advanced souls who normally reside in the higher Worlds and oversee the development of humanity. When a particular civilisation has reached its peak, it begins to wither. At such times this Blessed Company makes sure that its fruits are saved for the next season. One example is the Dark Ages when certain institutions preserved the knowledge of the past. The new flower was the Renaissance.

The head of the Holy Council and the spiritual hierarchy is Enoch who was the first fully self-realised individual. He was transfigured into Metatron who is still human but with archangelic powers. He is said to be privy to the Holy One's plans because he has a long-term overview of history.

The Messiah is the head of incarnate humanity. Some say that the Messiah came in the past, others that he is yet to come. The kabbalistic view is that there is always an Anointed present on the Earth holding the connection between humanity and Divinity. A Messiah can be a man or a woman and incarnated into any tradition. The Sufis call him the Axis of the Age. Most are hidden but some have had a public mission like Moses, Jesus and the Buddha.

In every generation there are also the saints and sages who demonstrate spiritual principles in their lives. They can operate in any field of human affairs. They are the bodhisattvas who carry out what is needed for a particular time and place, under the supervision of Providence.

Scale

Figure 51—COSMIC CLOCK
Astrology dates back to the Middle East of biblical times. Abraham came from Ur which was called the "City of Astrologers". Observation and detailed records over centuries led to the recognition of celestial patterns like the twelve distinct areas of influence called the zodiac. It was noted that these principles not only generated the seasons but also epochs in history as well as the character of individuals and nations. (Halevi)

47. Zodiac

The motion of the cosmos as observed from the earth gave rise to astrology. It has been developed and refined over millennia and it is still being enriched by observation and new discoveries. The study of astrology usually begins with the twelve signs of the zodiac. Each sign is like a stained glass window which colours the influence of the Sun, Moon and the planets.

The spring and autumn Equinoxes and summer and winter Solstices mark turning points in the zodiacal cycle. A Cardinal sign begins a new phase which is maintained in a Fixed sign and then dissolved in a Mutable sign. Terrestrial processes follow this pattern as Nature and human beings respond to celestial influences.

Another way to study the zodiac is to contemplate the qualities of the Earth, Water, Air and Fire signs and their relationships. Each three signs belonging to the same element have much in common. Earth and Water signs have a harmonious relationship, as do Air and Fire but, for example, Water and Fire do not. The opposing sign can be seen as the "shadow" while the square is distinctly disharmonious.

Planetary rulers give a further insight into the nature of each sign. Where a planet rules two signs, one is said to be active and the other one passive. Later, since the discovery of the outer planets, they have been added as co-rulers to signs which correspond to their characteristics.

The overlay of the twelve mundane Houses in a horoscope is based upon the zodiacal system. For example, the first House has the quality of Aries. While the planets in signs describe the character of a person, the planets in Houses define a particular area in life where the influence will manifest. The art of astrology is to form an integrated synthesis of all the different, sometimes contradictory, details and factors that make up a horoscope.

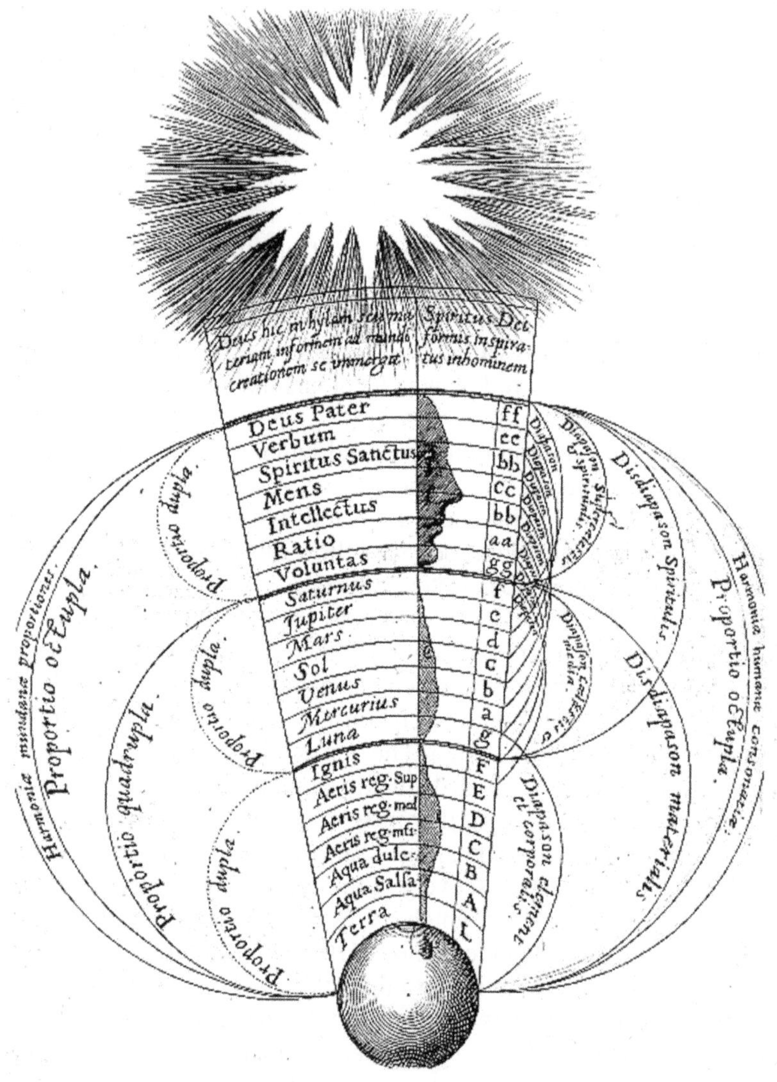

Figure 52—SPHERES

The geocentric view of the Solar system prevailed until about 400 years ago with Saturn as the outermost planet. Although the astronomical facts were not complete, people worked out how the macrocosm resonated with the microcosm. Some called it the music of the spheres. (Robert Fludd, 17th century)

48. *Solar System*

The Solar system is a living entity. Modern science is still putting together its history; how it was born and developed, where it is now and how it will die in a distant future. As technology and instruments improve, there is more detailed knowledge yet to be discovered.

The Sun is the centre that encompasses all the planets within its heliosphere. The gravity of the planets orbiting the Sun holds their moons in their positions. The whole Solar system moves around the galactic centre while the Milky Way has an even larger cycle.

Humanity has entered what is called the space age, exploring the Solar system and the wider universe. Landing on the Moon was a remarkable achievement. Now there are man-made satellites orbiting the earth, planets and the Sun on a mission to collect information at visible and invisible levels.

For example, the fluctuating sunspot cycle is known to affect electromagnetic fields and to influence organic life and human affairs. The solar maximum is seen to increase activity and productivity, while the minimum has the opposite effect. A kabbalist would consider the ebb and flow between the active and passive pillars at every level of Existence.

There are four ways to contemplate the Solar system; literal, symbolic, metaphysical and mystical. Astronomy provides the literal understanding. The symbolic way is to consider myths about planetary deities as the basis for interpreting astrology. The metaphysical aspect is revealed in relating the planets to the sefirot of the Tree of Life. A mystical experience can be an overview that includes all these levels in the Eternal Now.

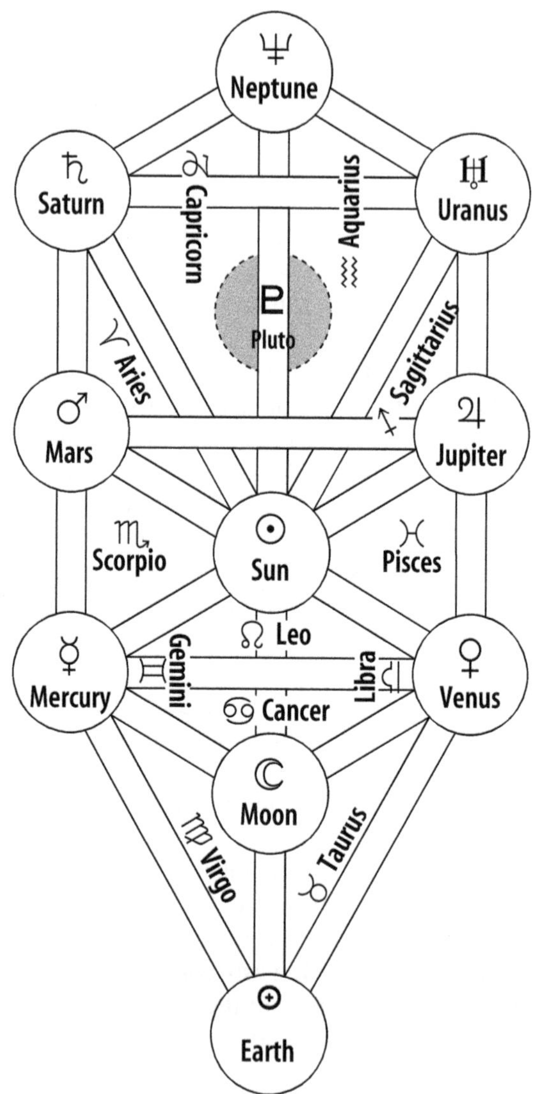

Figure 53—ASTROLOGY
Astrology is a symbolic science. Here the structure and dynamic of the Tree provide a cosmic framework while the planets and signs make up a mythology that defines the interaction between celestial principles. A parallel in modern science is the concept of frequencies, field forces and physical phenomena. (Halevi)

49. Horoscope

Traditional astrology depicts a horoscope in a circular form where the Sun, Moon and the planets are placed in the appropriate degree of a zodiacal sign. An experienced astrologer can perceive the pattern of a particular fate. This is determined by the interaction of the celestial configuration at the moment of birth. Thus the psyche is also called the astral body.

In kabbalistic astrology, the planetary principles are seen to correspond to the sefirotic functions of the Tree of Life. This gives a vertical dimension to a horoscope as one can perceive how the different levels of the psyche are influenced by the birth chart. The sign and House positions as well as aspects between planets are taken into account.

In a kabbalistic horoscope, the triads also resonate with the zodiacal signs that relate to their planetary rulers. For example, the "hands on" practical Earth signs of Taurus and Virgo are ruled by Venus and Mercury while the Earth sign of Capricorn, ruled by Saturn, is more concerned with long term plans.

Most people are psychologically asleep and do not fulfil their potential. They are either preoccupied with physicality according to their Ascendant at Malkhut or their social status governed by their Moon at Yesod. Those who are more awake start to individuate and live according to their Sun sign at Tiferet. Then their fate and the direction of their life become clearer.

The outer planets Uranus, Neptune and Pluto take several years to move through a particular sign. Thus a whole generation will have much in common in spite of individual differences. For example, the shared idealistic and esoteric values of the so called Flower Children of the 1960s reflect Neptune in Libra and Pluto in Leo in their horoscopes.

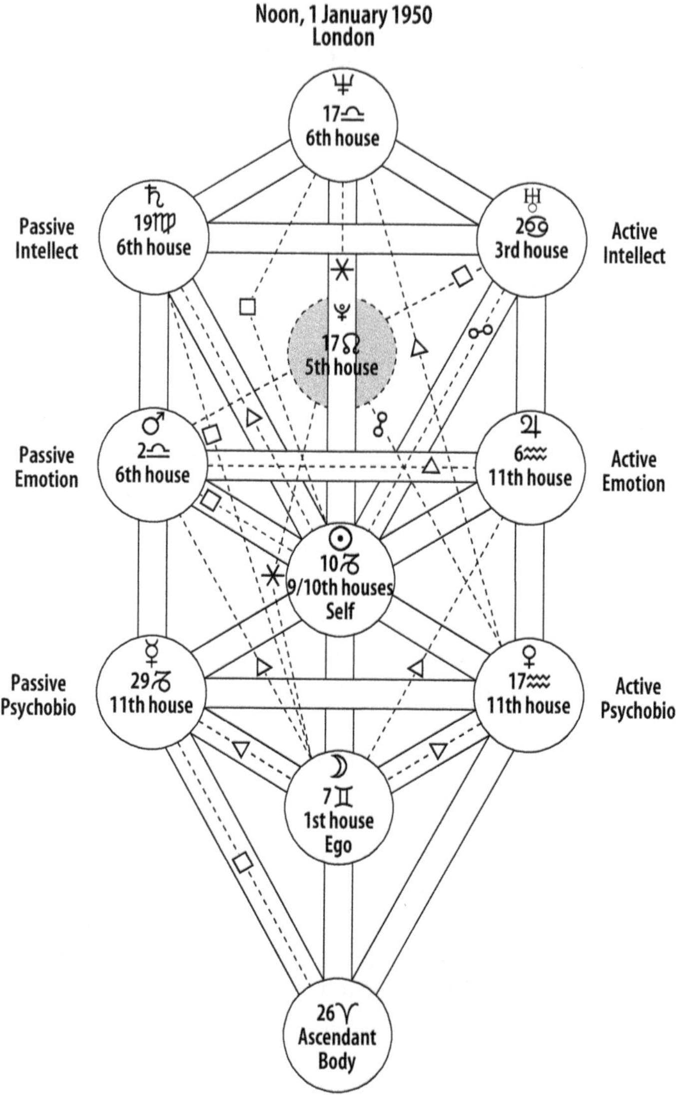

Figure 54—ASPECTS

Here a person's horoscope is superimposed on the Tree with the planetary positions related to their respective sefirot. The aspects between the planets/sefirot are taken into account. Sextiles and trines are considered harmonious while squares and oppositions are seen as hard aspects. It is also worth noting if there are no aspects between two planets. (Halevi)

50. *Tree Chart*

In this example, we begin analysing the horoscope by looking at the lower face of the Tree. The independence of the fiery Aries Ascendant/ Malkhut is under stress from the person's social life with Mercury/ Hod in the 11th House. The Yesod/ego Moon in Gemini in the 1st House would make him a good talker but this trickster element could get out of hand as there is no obvious connection between the ego and the Self. However, the easy flow from Hod and Nezah will make him popular amongst his many friends.

The Tiferet/Self is influenced by the Sun in Capricorn on the Midheaven which makes the person quite ambitious. The square to his Mars/Gevurah in the 6th House is likely to load him with overwork while the Jupiter/Hesed trine to Mars will provide the energy to carry out his plans. He would be interested in politics and organising and may well finish up in a prominent position.

His transpersonal contribution could be in analytical detail with his Saturn/Binah in the 6th House and original insights with Uranus/ Hokhmah in the 3rd House. The square from his Neptune/Keter to his Sun does not incline him to seek conventional religion but the Neptune trine to Venus might give mystical experiences while enjoying the arts or the beauty of Nature.

While the natal horoscope gives an outline of a person's fate, one also needs to consider how it relates to the current celestial situation. A particular transit can activate or block a certain planetary/sefirotic principle for a short or a long period creating good or bad times. Progressions are based on the idea that one 24-hour cycle after birth corresponds to a whole year in later life. This person might change from a conservative Capricorn to a radical Aquarius at the age of 20 and later into an introvert Pisces at 50. Thus there are cycles within cycles in the fluidic realm of the psyche.

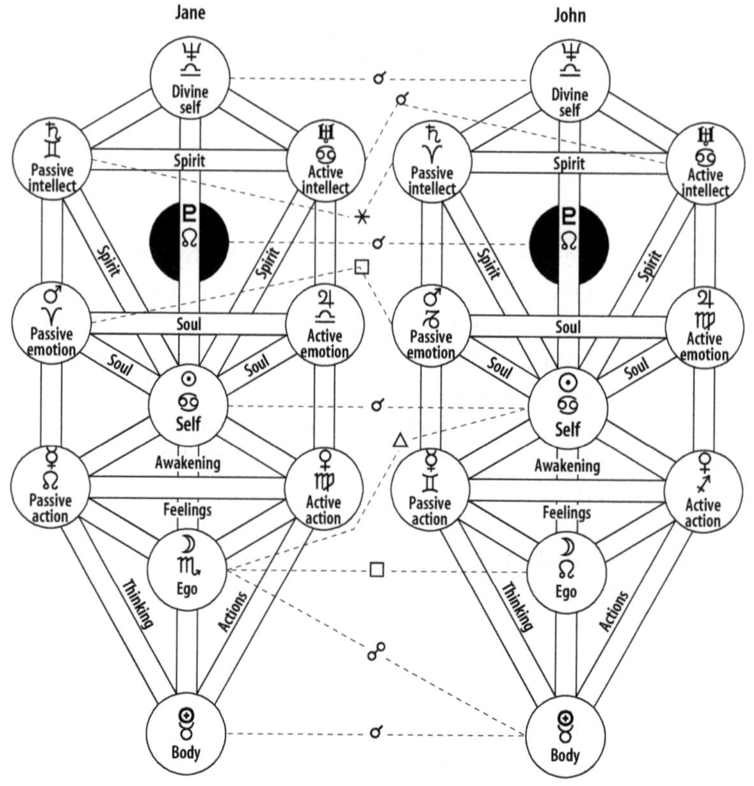

Figure 55—CHEMISTRY

The proverbs about human relationships say that like is drawn to like or that opposites attract each other. That is quite common when comparing the horoscopes of a couple. However, there is also a more subtle astrological chemistry at work between people. It depends on their level of awareness and maturity how well they can negotiate their differences. (Halevi)

51. Connections

Most encounters in human society are quite neutral, based on correct behaviour according to local culture. There needs to be a certain chemistry between people to form intimate relationships. If there is a karmic connection, even a short meeting can become life changing.

If John and Jane in our example are young people looking for a romance, they would find each other attractive because they both have a sensuous Taurus body type. There would also be a good resonance between their Suns in watery Cancer. However, their Moons are squared to each other which can indicate very different backgrounds and a difficulty in understanding each other at the social level. With their Cancer Suns and a square between their Mars, the relationship may end in manipulative power games and quarrels.

However, if John is the father and Jane the daughter, then the relationship is for a lifetime. John's Sun in Cancer would feel naturally protective towards Jane, particularly because his Sun is trine to her Moon. When she grows up, his flamboyant Leo Moon would criticise her Scorpio Moon for being too introvert and timid. Her impulsive Mars in Aries would find his Capricorn Mars discipline too restrictive and she would rebel, probably secretly in true Scorpionic fashion while her Cancer Sun would hold on to the family security. There is often a common astrological theme running through families indicating karmic connections.

A marriage is like an alchemical retort which can have a transformative effect on both individuals. It is not uncommon that a person seeks to compensate for a lack of a certain element in their own horoscope by finding a partner to fulfil the role. Knowing each other's astrological type and horoscope in detail would help people to compromise and find a middle ground based on consciousness instead of just reacting.

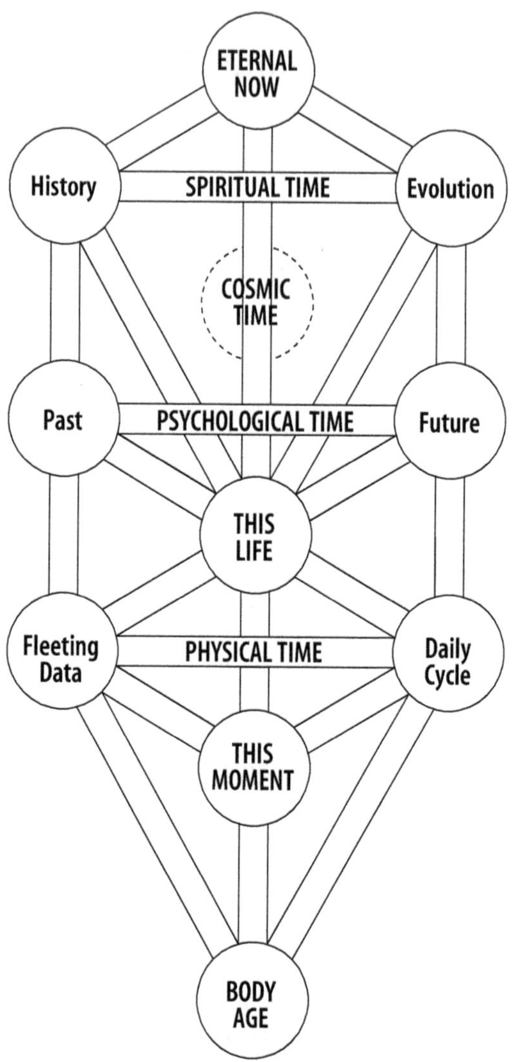

Figure 56—CHRONOLOGY

Human perception of time depends on circumstance and level of awareness. An infant's experience is quite different from that of an old person. A musician is acutely aware of precise timing while a scholar may consider a whole historical epoch. There is an objective way to measure physical time, sometimes called the ticktock time, which is a useful reference point. To lose one's sense of time can be a sign of a psychological disorder. (Halevi)

52. Recollection

When one is born, what happened in past lives comes with the soul into the present incarnation. Such memories are stored in the unconscious and have an effect on each new life. The outline of the future is already set in the person's horoscope but it is not yet actuality. As the future unfolds, it becomes the past and eventually the present life becomes another past life memory.

A phenomenon called déjà vu can relate to a past life. It is not uncommon that one encounters someone who seems strangely familiar. If it is mutual, such an experience may indicate a karmic connection or a spiritual companionship from a previous life. This order of recognition happens at the soul level. Some people have a similar experience when visiting a place like an old town where they may have lived before or they may feel at home in a foreign country.

This Tree shows how different orders of time are present within one incarnation. A human lifetime is limited and therefore timing is crucial. Certain things are appropriate, for example, only in childhood. If one is out of sequence and remains childish in adulthood, that will create problems. At the individual level, each person has their own schedule provided by astrological transits and progressions which may occur only once in a lifetime.

The movement of time can be perceived as linear between a beginning and an end, repeating cycles or spirals or even vertical in the moment Now. History goes to the collective memory of a people and evolution is preserved in the memory of species and the planet. Esoteric traditions speak of akashic records where everything that has taken place is preserved in cosmic time. Such records are accessible to advanced individuals who have reached the level of prophecy or enlightenment.

Figure 57—SUNDIAL
This sculpture on the wall of a medieval church depicts the Angel of Time. The sundial counts the daylight hours while the night can be seen as the unconscious dream time. Occasionally, however, moonlight can illuminate the sundial generating a different perspective. (Drawing by Halevi)

53. *Impressions*

If one spends some time in an old graveyard, it can be thought-provoking as one observes several layers of time present there. First the past is inevitably evoked but so too is the present. One may consider one's own mortality and Eternity as well as being reminded of the purpose of Existence.

Evidence of geological time is visible in surrounding gravestones. Marble was once fluidic which is recorded in its patterns. The old polished granite slabs have lost their pristine surface. They are continuously eroding as the seasons, climate change and lichen take their toll.

A man walking his dog and passing by is an example of the history of evolution. The man carries genes of his prehistoric ancestors while his pedigree dog is related to wolves. Familiar flowers and trees were once a novelty on this planet and what is seen now is the result of a long chain of transformations in form and substance.

Every grave tells a story of a human lifetime. What happened between the dates of birth and death recorded on the tombstone may or may not have been a fulfilled life. There are many views of afterlife from Heaven and Paradise to Hell. However, some people believe just in oblivion.

In the kabbalistic view, we have left many gravestones behind in our previous incarnations. Although we may not remember our past lives, they are deeply engraved in the fabric of the soul in the unconscious. A contemplation or meditation in a cemetery may stimulate old memories, give insights into the "passing show" and highlight the preciousness of the moment Now.

Psychology

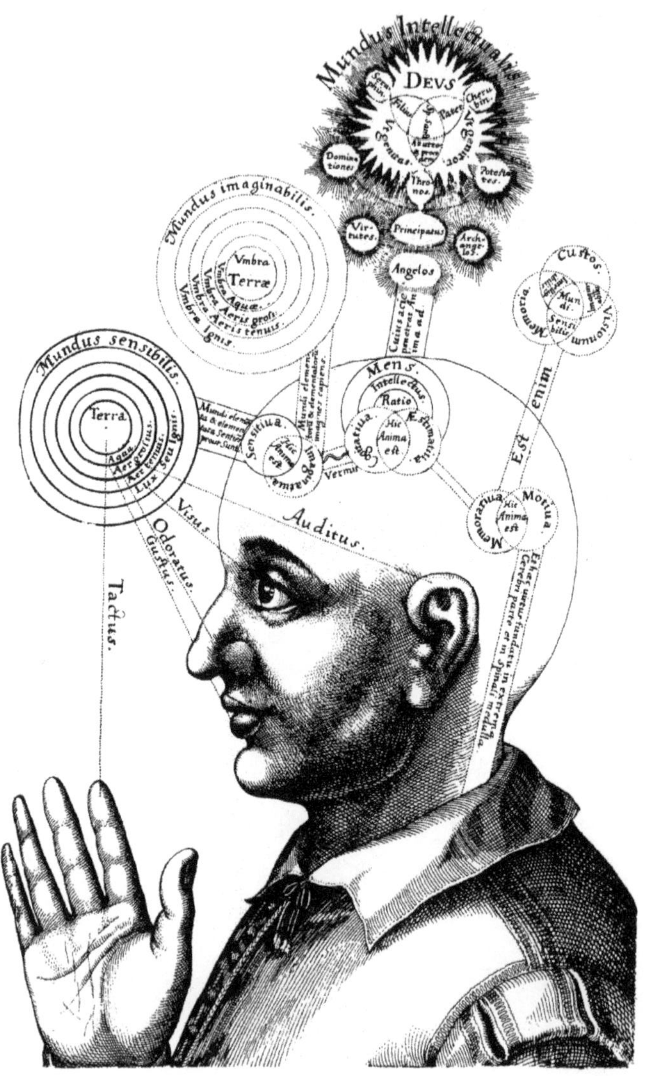

Figure 58—KNOWLEDGE

One can acquire knowledge externally through physical senses and internally through higher consciousness, as symbolised by the kabbalistic Tree above. In the middle zone of the psyche knowledge is processed through analysis, synthesis and imagination. (Robert Fludd, 17th century)

54. Microcosm

Each human being is a microcosm of Existence containing a spark of Adam Kadmon, a spirit, a psyche and a physical body. The psyche is immortal, that is, it survives death and continues its journey in the process of reincarnation.

The nature of the psyche is fluidic and changeable. However, there are some permanent characteristics that are very difficult to change in a lifetime, if at all. Since ancient times, people have observed and tried to classify some common features of these deep currents as different types. Often there is a distinct connection between the body type and psychological tendencies.

Hippocrates (c.400 B.C.E.) observed that there were four different body fluids or humours. These produced four temperaments called sanguine, phlegmatic, melancholic and choleric. Usually one of these elements is predominant creating a particular type, although all of them are present to a greater or lesser degree. In ancient India, Ayurveda had a similar classification.

The zodiacal division into twelve types of humanity is more psychological although the subdivision into elements takes into account physical qualities. Thus the Earth signs are described as stocky and muscular, Air signs tall and thin, Water signs soft and plump and the Fire signs strong and energetic. Another way is to observe people's natural inclinations to be either doers, thinkers or feelers.

The beginning of psychological development is to recognise one's own type and to make a conscious effort to balance off any excessive tendencies. Whatever the categorisation, all types have the possibility to raise their level from mineral, vegetable and animal to becoming fully human.

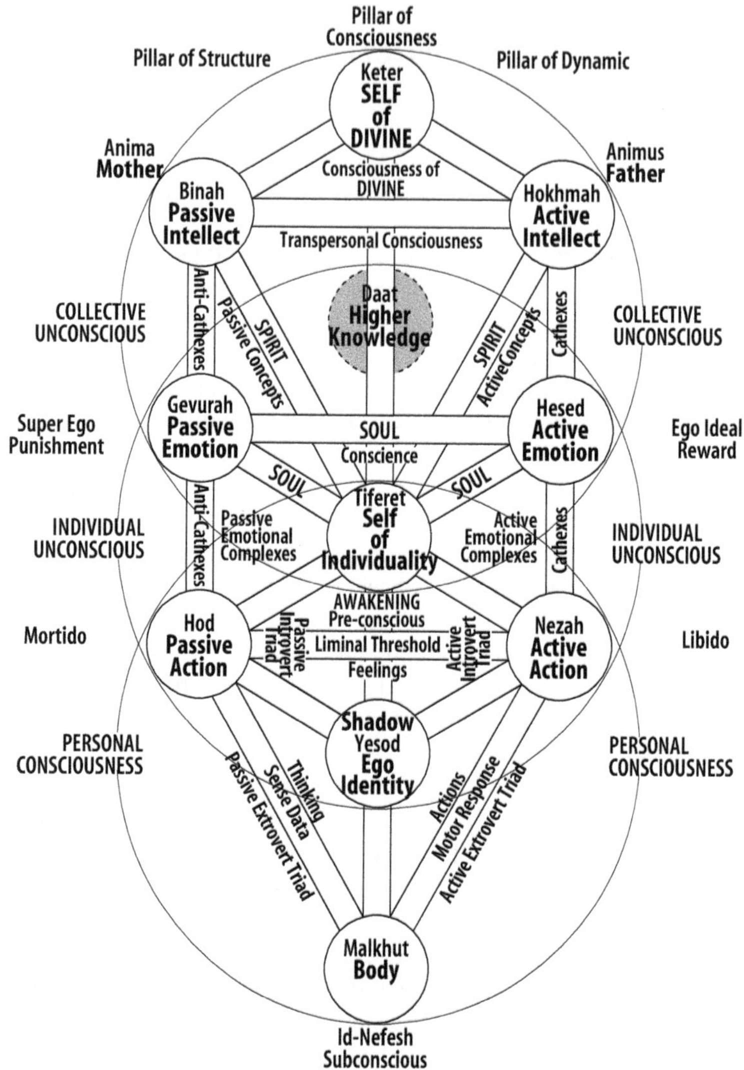

Figure 59—ANATOMY

The principles of the sefirotic Tree can be applied to the psyche which is a Yeziratic entity. The dynamic and the structure of the outer pillars manifest as active and passive functions, whereas the central pillar with its sefirot and triads relates to different levels of consciousness. The paths facilitate flow and interaction within the psyche. At the centre is the soul, the agent of free will. (Halevi)

55. Psyche

The psyche has access to all four Worlds. The lower part interacts with the body while the more subtle upper face relates to the spirit and its Keter touches the Divine. The key element is the central pillar of consciousness.

The lower face of personal consciousness is centred in Yesod/ego. Here is the arena of the everyday awareness of action, thinking and feeling as well as dealing with the external world. How this part of the psyche is trained and conditioned will manifest as the persona or the ego's sense of identity. The body's instincts and drives remain largely hidden in the subconscious, unless something in particular needs attention, but they have an influence on a person's behaviour.

At the centre of the individual unconscious is the Self in Tiferet where the three lower Worlds meet. This Watcher is usually unnoticed until the person is woken up by some important incident and becomes aware of their soul. The soul triad is the area of free will where important decisions are made. The memories and experience in the emotional and intellectual complexes of the side triads act as a psychological frame of reference.

The zone of collective unconscious is transpersonal although it can manifest through individuals. It contains various archetypes that form a person's world view as well as the mood of the time which affects whole societies. The three higher Worlds meet at Keter where one may have a glimpse of the purpose of Existence.

The anatomy of the psyche contains all these components but the centre of gravity and emphasis are variable in the fluidic World of Forms. There is always oscillation between active and passive tendencies with the central pillar of consciousness seeking equilibrium.

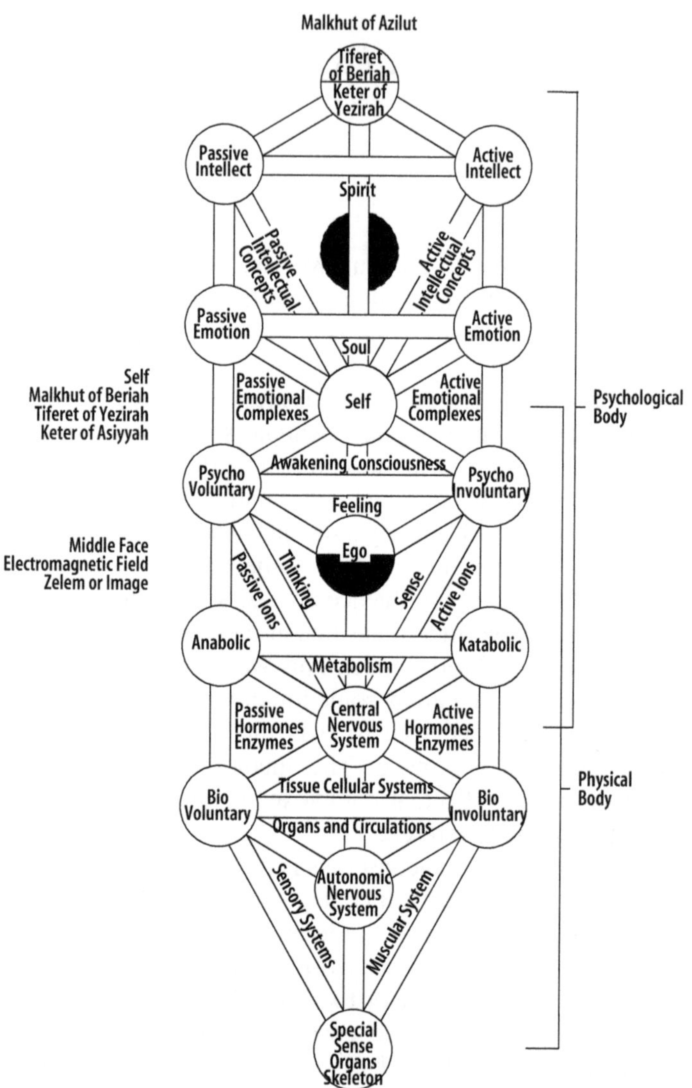

Figure 60—CONNECTIONS

The body and the psyche resonate with each other. The main area of interaction is between the upper face of the body and the lower face of the psyche. What is below the central nervous system is purely biological and beyond conscious control. The Daat of the body relates to the everyday mind of the ego while the level of peak experience at the physical Keter may touch the psychological Self and the Kingdom of Heaven. (Halevi)

56. Subconscious

In Kabbalah, the term "subconscious" means influences that are below everyday consciousness, in contrast to "unconscious" which refers to the higher levels of Jacob's Ladder above. The subconscious contains the body's instinctive intelligence and the drive for survival. The mortido and libido impulses of the left and right pillars can have a strong influence on the psyche unless controlled by the central pillar of consciousness.

The subconscious also holds many acquired skills. For example, learning to ride a bicycle or to drive a car requires at first much conscious attention from the ego. When the sequence of actions has been repeated many times, it becomes part of the knowledge of the body. In the long run, the autonomic nervous system will be in charge of the operation. This frees the lower mind to think about something else while performing routine actions.

However, if something out of the ordinary is about to go wrong, the subconscious will alert the ego, for example, to check a peculiar noise coming from the vehicle. Or if a sudden danger appears, instinctive reflexes take over to avoid an accident. The subconscious mind has its own watcher which is always observing what is going on in the environment.

The subconscious is also the area of psychosomatic interaction. One's psychological state has a strong influence on the well-being of the body and vice versa. If the warnings are being ignored, the body may become ill. Sometimes planetary transits affect the body, for example, in periods of stress or ease.

The psychosomatic "feel good" factor can be a double-edged sword as it can incline a person to repeat a pleasurable experience. This can lead to excesses like overeating or even harmful addictions. It takes much experience and sensitivity to find a healthy balance.

Figure 61—SELF

The qualities of Tiferet are Truth, Goodness and Beauty. This refers to the three components of the Self; Malkhut of Beriah or the spirit, Tiferet of Yezirah or the psyche and the Keter of Asiyyah or the body. One archetypal symbol is the Sun with its central position. It is also called the Seat of Solomon as the Self is both the watcher and the ruler of the psyche. The Self represents the essence of one's individuality, in contrast to the outer ego persona symbolised by the Moon. (Robert Fludd, 17th century)

57. Unconscious

Most people are largely psychologically asleep because their focus is centred in the ego which runs the routines of life. These are current preoccupations as well as daydreams. Such activities take place within the great vegetable triad. Above the subliminal threshold of Hod-Nezah is the unconscious.

Sometimes individuals do wake up as a result of an unusual event but usually this does not last. It takes much effort to shift one's centre of gravity to the Self. When that does happen, the quality of life changes as the psyche becomes more integrated. However, some people who have attained this degree of Self-consciousness choose to use it to exploit others who are still asleep. Then there is no further development if the warnings of the conscience are being ignored.

The unconscious contains the memories of this lifetime and previous ones. Most of them are quite neutral and form a general cultural background. Some memories which are highly charged with pain or pleasure cluster together to form emotional complexes. These can have a strong influence on a person's behaviour and attitudes as do many collective concepts of reward or punishment. One needs to examine these hidden factors so that they are not allowed to dominate one's life.

Not only the past but also the potential of the future is stored here. The unconscious is always trying to guide the individual towards fulfilling their fate and destiny. Its language is symbolic through dreams, omens and coincidences to draw one's attention to what is needed. The unconscious is an enormous resource in the process of individuation.

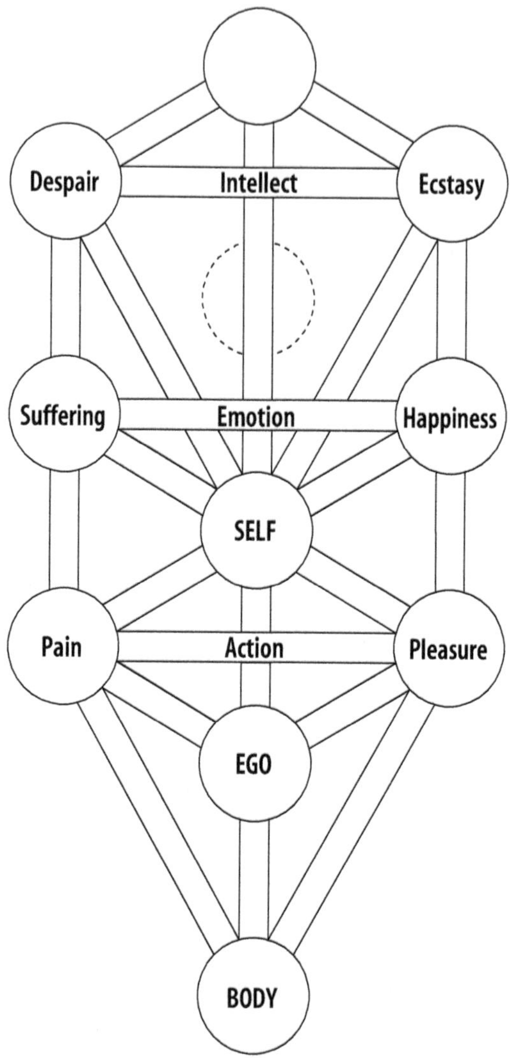

Figure 62—EXTREMES
As there are psychological storms due to cosmic weather or personal problems, one may encounter extreme conditions. Here it is important to remember that they do pass and clear skies and sunshine will reappear. If one is centred in the Self, then one can monitor and moderate most extremes. (Halevi)

58. Polarities

Pain and pleasure are part of everyday life. They are the tools of conditioning, "stick and carrot", as most people want to avoid pain and seek pleasure. Pain is also a signal that warns about danger while pleasure can reflect the vitality of a healthy organism.

When one begins to develop and wants to achieve something, one's attitudes need to change. For example, learning a new skill may require much practice and enduring physical or even psychological stress. If one just wants to avoid pain at any cost, it can result in stagnation. Also, one's pleasures may need to change to something more refined if one wants to shift levels.

The soul level awakens the conscience. Past errors need to be acknowledged, often by suffering remorse before the issue is released. Suffering can also teach discipline and fortitude in dealing with difficulties. Happiness is the active function of the soul and it gives the psyche a certain radiance. For many it is the aim of their interior work but the process should not stop there.

Increasing understanding can sometimes lead to a deep despair when one sees the inevitability of transpersonal events. Such a test can put a person off the spiritual path. In contrast, a moment of revelation can be ecstatic when one transcends the limitations of the rational mind. Inspiration is a necessary part of a creative intellectual process.

The scale of these polarities is not black and white as there are many shades in between. It is inherent in the nature of the Tree that it seeks to correct any imbalance by swinging towards the opposite pole. This oscillation is observed by the Self or "the Watcher" which can intervene when necessary, holding the central pillar of consciousness steady.

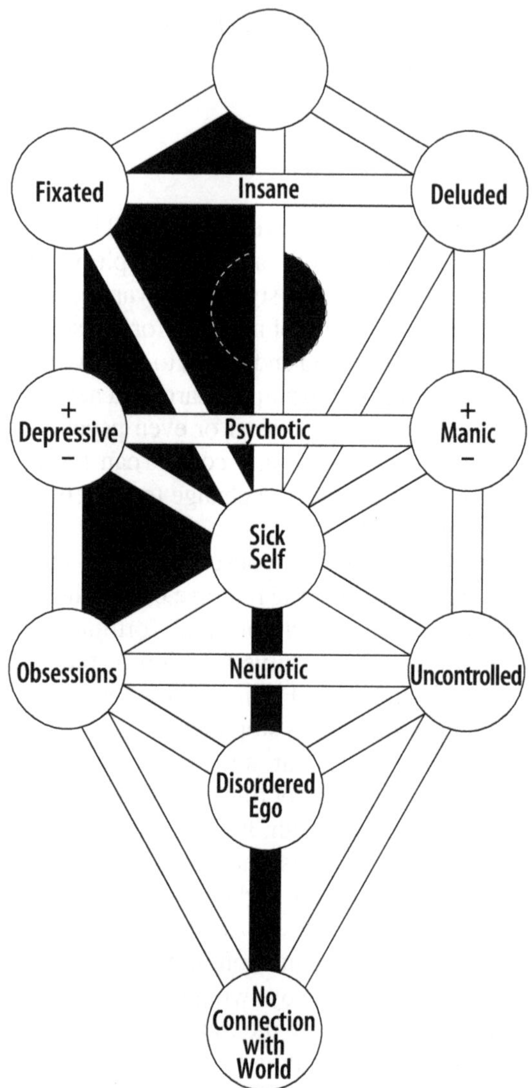

Figure 63—PATHOLOGY

It has been observed that animals can become neurotic or go mad in distressing circumstances. So can human beings. Some individuals may even become psychotic or insane while whole nations can have a nervous breakdown as seen in revolutions or religious wars. In this example, the psyche is overloaded on one side which can be a transient episode or a permanent condition. (Halevi)

59. *Disorders*

Psychological illnesses are not new. Since ancient times, people have tried to understand the causes of madness and find treatments. The ritualistic exorcising of evil spirits was not uncommon until the advent of modern science. The study of genetic, chemical and environmental factors behind mental illness became the norm until psychotherapy was introduced. A kabbalistic practitioner may use the sefirotic Tree as a diagnostic tool to define the zones of affliction.

Most conditions are based on a weak or distorted ego which can diminish the functions of action, thinking and feeling. It is not always due to deprivation in childhood conditioning but too much money and privilege that can also trap a person in their private dream world. Many lunatics living in their fantasies are considered as no more than harmless eccentrics.

The more serious mental conditions can oscillate between depression and mania if the individual is not centred in the Self. Sometimes psychotic tendencies are not immediately obvious as some intelligent people with an inflated Self can radiate a certain charismatic power. If they are in an influential position in their society they can be dangerous, for example leading a whole nation into a disaster. People who are permanently insane have lost touch with reality. Often they become incapable of looking after themselves and need to be in an institution.

Sefirotic and astrological principles contain powerful positive and negative archetypes. Some individuals can become obsessed or possessed by them. Another form of possession can be an external discarnate entity who seeks to gain access to an imbalanced psyche. Fortunately most people are protected by the archetype of health and normality.

Figure 64—DIAGNOSIS

Up to the 18th century, it was not uncommon for a physician to consult astrology in diagnosis and prescribing remedies. In this way a traditional healer takes into account not only the physical condition of the patient but the current influence of the cosmos. For example, the phases of the Moon are known to affect the body fluids. Since the 1960s, the New Age movement has revived many old healing methods and developed new ones. (16th century print)

60. Healing

The archangel Raphael, whose name means the Healer of God, represents the Hod principle in the World of Creation. As such, it is the creative method of analysing and understanding a problem and then choosing a treatment. In the body, the immune system is a healing mechanism that checks and corrects any imbalance in order to maintain optimum health. Sometimes, however, a person becomes so ill that they have to seek external help.

An experienced healer will look at the patient's general state of being as well as particular symptoms. The origin of the illness may be physical, psychological or spiritual or a combination of these. The nature of the illness can be transitory, long-term or incurable. The solution may include physical treatment or specific remedies.

Psychotherapy is a treatment for a wide range of mental disorders. However, no therapist can offer a cure without the active participation of the client who has to make the effort to change. The healer's position is often between Hesed and Gevurah as their help can include comments that the client finds too severe.

A spiritual crisis may occur, for example, if a person cannot reconcile conflicting views. A serious denial may lead to atrophy if the rejuvenating influence of the higher Worlds is blocked. In contrast, a spiritual intervention can enable the individual to recover. This can manifest in a miraculous cure, if it is willed from above.

A skilful practitioner will consult the client's horoscope. For example, a planetary transit may be quite short or last for months. This can give an insight into a difficult epoch in one's fate and the confidence to endure it until the affliction passes.

Figure 65—DREAMS

Upon falling asleep one enters another reality where physical laws do not apply. The unconscious uses symbols and archetypes which, if understood, can carry an important message to the dreamer. Here, for example, the ship of the soul is moving towards the Light and the higher levels of the psyche. Such a dream may present a shift away from the dark cliffs and a sinister looking raven that symbolise a problem. (19th century engraving)

61. Sleep

A third of a lifetime is spent physically asleep. This allows the body to relax and heal. Meanwhile the ego retreats into the unconscious to review immediate and long term processes. Some of these are displayed on the screen of Yesod as dreams.

Daydreaming is a form of psychological sleep that can lead to trivial or obsessive fantasies. In contrast, conscious or active imagination can use dreaming in a creative way. Many artists and inventors apply this method. The expression, 'to sleep on it' is to make good use of both personal and collective unconscious.

Most dreams are routine psychological processes. However, if a dream comes from the deep level of the unconscious, it has a distinct quality. There is a lucid clarity when the Tiferet/Self is present. Such a dream is often so vivid that it can be recalled even years later. It is usually concerned with one's development or it can be a prophetic insight into a collective situation.

When analysing a dream, one needs to take into account the actual life situation at that point in time. For example, the image of a baby may be a biological wish while for an older person it may symbolise a new creative idea. Dreaming about water may give an insight into one's feelings and emotions. Gevurah can manifest in nightmares while Hesed would give hope and encouragement.

In a dream, familiar people or strangers can represent subpersonalities or archetypes. As such, they can be messengers from any level of Jacob's Ladder.

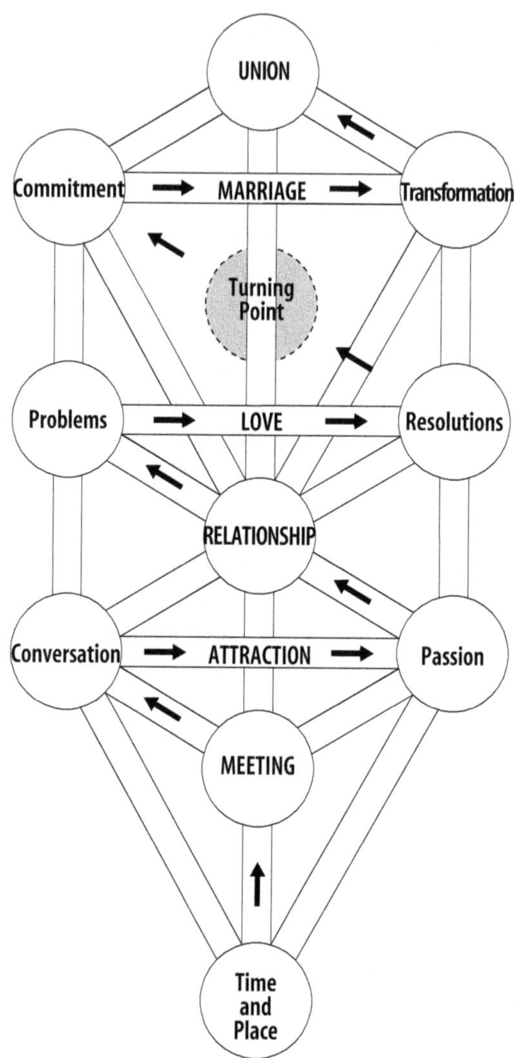

Figure 66—MARRIAGE

It is said that marriages are made in Heaven. Such an idea implies that a marriage can be preordained for karmic reasons. Some unions are even destined to have a special and transpersonal purpose. However, not all marriages are of this order and not all relationships lead to a good marriage. Many are experiments that can end in separation. (Halevi)

62. *Relationships*

One of the great human preoccupations is to find a suitable partner. The dream is to find the ideal love match but underneath this impulse is the biological desire for procreation and the continuity of the family and clan. At the vegetable level, this instinctive drive is all powerful as men and women seek to make themselves attractive to the opposite sex. Fashions change but not the basic need for home and security.

Animal level people are more selective as alpha males want alpha females and vice versa to enhance their status and power. Such liaisons are often based more on class and wealth than compatibility or love. Behind appearances, a trophy wife may be deeply unhappy. A proverb says, "Whoever marries for money has to work for it".

Love at first sight is a powerful experience. It can mean recognising a partner from a previous life. However, often it is more about falling in love with one's animus or anima archetype. Such a relationship may be very romantic to begin with but, if the reality does not fulfil one's expectations, the projection can shift to somebody else.

People at the human level seek to find a soul companion who would understand their inner life. Many individuals prefer to live alone rather than compromise their ideal. However, it is possible to have a good working marriage if, for example, the prospective partners are under the same spiritual discipline or share a harmonious astrological configuration.

Be it a good or a bad match, a marriage has a transformative effect on both partners. It can be either a pressure cooker or an alchemical retort depending on the level of inner development. If successful, the result is a strong team that can play an important part in a society.

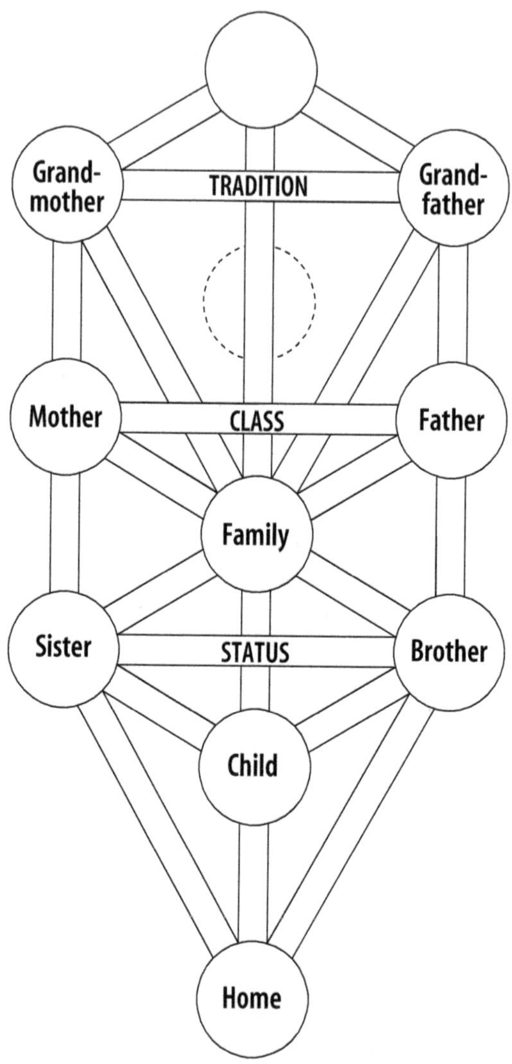

Figure 67—FAMILY
An individual begins life as a child of a particular family which is part of their cultural foundation for that lifetime. On reaching maturity, most usually start their own family. Thus the family tree will grow new branches with the in-laws and their clan added to it. Such networks can form the basis of a tribe, society or a nation. (Halevi)

63. Roles

Family roles are archetypal. If any of these positions is not present in one's upbringing, a person may seek to compensate for it later in life. An only child can bond with a friend in order to have a brother or a sister. If one grows up without a father or a mother, one may instinctively seek the company of older people. In a normal family, one's relationship with one's parents and siblings is important as it also sets out the patterns of how one connects with other people.

In a lifetime, one may fill several of these roles. One will always remain the child of one's parents while simultaneously being a mother or father to one's own children. Many people enjoy the role of a grandparent. What stories the grandparents can tell about their own lives are still within living memory, before passing to history and the background of general family tradition.

Each family has its emphasis depending on its status and class in a society. Moreover, different family members can be at the vegetable, animal or human level of development. A child may be an old soul while the parent can be juvenile. All these combinations form a particular family life.

Those who begin to individuate seek the company of like-minded people outside the family, often to encounter archetypal family roles in another form. For example, many spiritual organisations call their members Brothers and Sisters. That may be just a convention or a genuine bond between people belonging to the same discipline. In a spiritual hierarchy there are also Mothers and Fathers who are usually more mature people caring for and teaching the younger ones. Those who become the Elders of a tradition fulfil the role of grandparents providing wisdom and understanding.

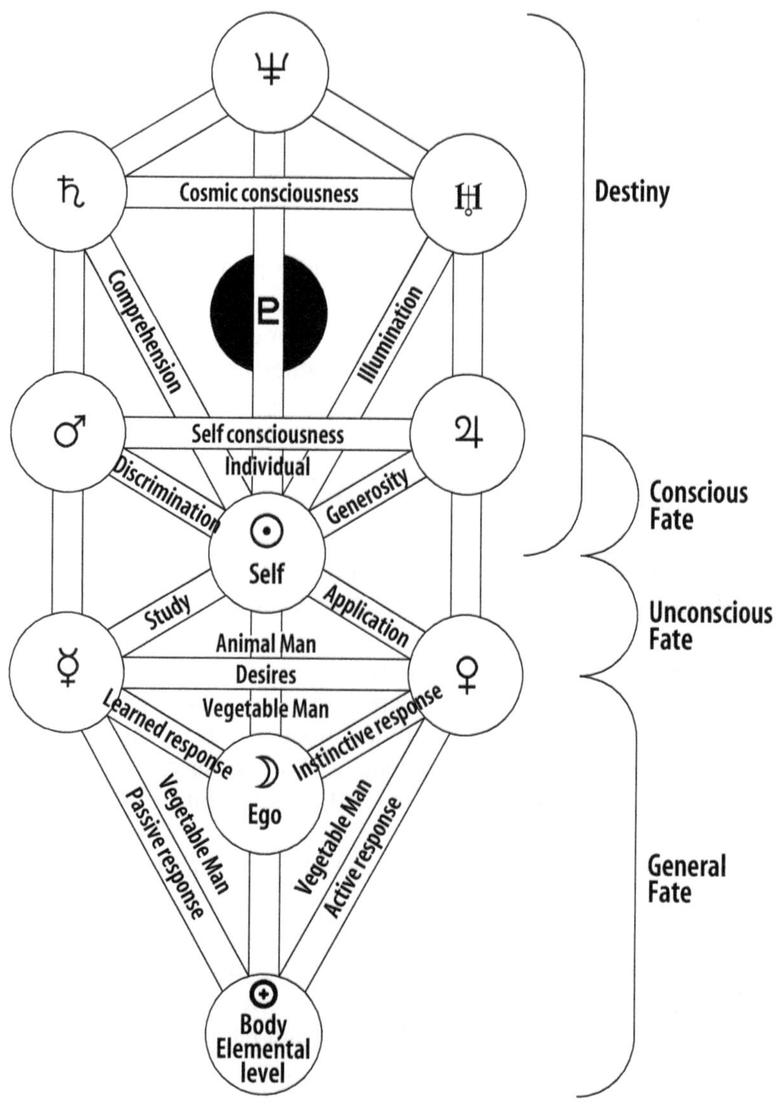

Figure 68—FATE AND DESTINY
It has been debated for centuries whether fate is fixed or not. Some say it is preordained while others take into account human free will. The kabbalistic view is that fate is partly determined by the karma of previous lives but every new incarnation has certain potential to be fulfilled. (Halevi)

64. Choices

The driving force of most people is the vegetable need for security and social pressure from their family and peers. They are inclined to conform to the current modes and values of their society. They are part of the masses and as such they come under the law of large numbers or general fate. They may even be talented and skilled but their centre of gravity is their ego and their fortunes depend on external circumstances like political and economic fluctuations.

Animal level people are more enterprising. They are on the lookout for opportunities and they make the effort to follow them up. They stand out in a crowd and may become influential and powerful. However, if they are unaware of the compulsions that drive them, their inner life may remain empty or confused. That is often when people wake up and start asking deeper questions and seeking answers.

Self-conscious individuals may not be conspicuous but they have an inner strength that is not dependent on others. Such people are aware of their souls and know their life's purpose. Sometimes they struggle against all the odds to fulfil their fate.

People of destiny can make a contribution to human evolution with their experience and vision. It may be in practical inventions, arts and sciences or spiritual movements. For example, the Maharishi brought the Transcendental Meditation to the West in the 1960s which was one of the inspirations for the New Age.

In their old age, people see the fruits of their life and reflect on the choices they made. Often they regret what they did not do while mistakes and errors are accepted as learning experiences. Revelations may come about how one's own fate is interwoven with that of other people, making a distinct pattern in the tapestry of history.

Systems

Figure 69—MIRROR

For millennia, human beings have endeavoured to understand the totality of Existence. The 17th century European intelligentsia studied not only biblical theology but the Hellenic tradition and Kabbalah. This composite image depicts the ordered unity of the four Worlds as a mirror of Existence with the Divine connection reaching through all levels via the symbol of the feminine principle of the Shekhinah. (Robert Fludd, 17th century)

65. *Influences*

Most sacred art is either devotional or contemplative. The devotional approach presents spiritual principles in symbolic forms while the contemplative mode uses metaphysical concepts in its imagery. For example, most traditional icons were designed to appeal to the heart. They were carefully constructed according to certain evocative formulae where every detail had a specific meaning from hand gestures to the haloes of the saints. As such they became signposts to the Heavens.

With the advent of printed books and translations of classical and esoteric texts, the intellectual dimension was opened and people were able to study a wide variety of topics from different sources. The Neoplatonic model together with Kabbalah inspired esotericists to formulate metaphysical views that depicted the universal Chain of Being and the microcosm of Man. These graphic images were widely studied in Europe outside the religious establishment.

Artists are sometimes called 'lesser prophets' because they are sensitive to the influences of the higher Worlds. With knowledge of a metaphysical framework, their insights can produce works that combine the intellectual and symbolic approaches into a mystical presentation. Verbal images can be just as powerful as visual ones. The words of some poets are being read and contemplated even hundreds of years later.

With the Age of Reason, metaphysical and esoteric studies went out of fashion but continued discreetly within the schools of the soul. Modern science has expanded the physical world-view which in turn has enriched the esoteric view of Existence.

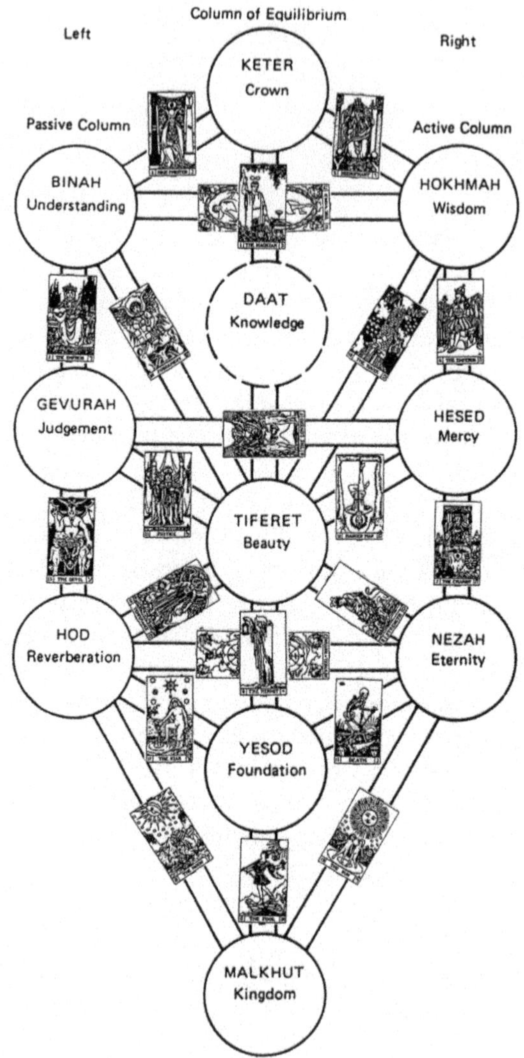

Figure 70—TAROT

The word 'Tarot', in Hebrew, means 'Teachings'. This graphic set of cards is based on the kabbalistic framework of four Worlds and ten sefirot of the Tree with its twenty-two paths. It also includes within its system the symbolism of two parallel esoteric lines, Hermeticism and Alchemy. The obscure format of a card game was to disguise an occult or hidden Teaching from the Inquisition. (Tarot on the Tree, source unknown)

66. Correspondences

A pack of ordinary playing cards has four suits representing the four Worlds, ten cards within each suit relating to the ten sefirot of each World and four court cards defining four levels within each suit/World. A pack of Tarot cards has the same division within its Minor Arcana but it also has twenty-two picture cards called Major Arcana. These are related to the twenty-two paths of the Tree and the twenty-two letters of the Hebrew alphabet. However, there is no universal agreement about these correspondences and there are several variations in existence.

The Tarot suits depict Existence in a symbolic form. In this system, the Pentacles relate to the mundane physical World while the Cups are containers for the fluidic World of Forms and the psyche. The Swords represent the spiritual World. The Wands or Torches symbolise the fire of the Divine World. The court cards use the medieval ranks of page, knight, queen and king to illustrate these fourfold principles.

The Major Arcana set out the story of development and transformation. Beginning from the innocence of the Fool, one gains wisdom and understanding through various experiences. For example, one may achieve worldly or even spiritual power for a while but then a disaster can strike in the form of a Falling Tower. In essence, the images depict archetypal processes in life.

Unfortunately, over time the Tarot has become a device for fortune-telling instead of a metaphysical system. The Tarot's power is that the cards appeal to the intellectual aspect of imagination. The symbols may give profound insights if used as a tool for contemplation.

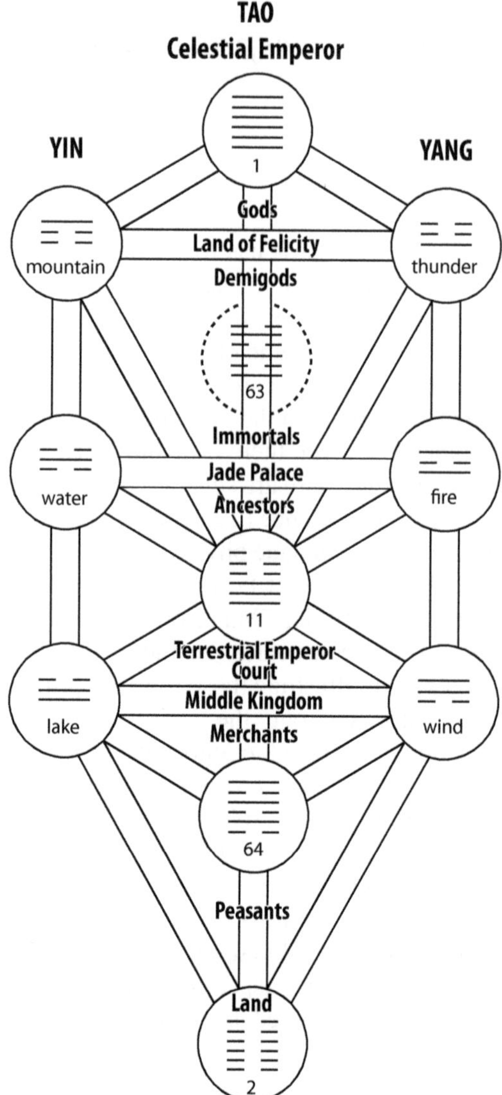

Figure 71—I CHING

The Chinese classic I Ching began as an oracle in shamanistic prehistory. Over time, this Book of Changes was developed into a universal political, psychological and metaphysical system. For example, the central hexagram Peace takes the Tiferet position halfway between Heaven and Earth. The trigram Water has a strong Yang line contained between two constricting Yin lines at Gevurah while the expansive trigram Fire is at Hesed. Together they compose the soul triad. (Halevi)

67. Yang-Yin

The I Ching uses an unbroken line (—) as a symbol for Yang and a broken line (– –) for Yin. In kabbalistic terms, these can be seen as the right and left pillars or the upper and lower faces of the Tree of Life. This polarity manifests in complementaries like active and passive, light and dark or masculine and feminine principles.

According to this esoteric system, everything that exists is based on eight fundamental principles called trigrams. These introduce a middle line between the Yang and Yin polarity which acts as a third force. As such, these three factors are perceived as positive, negative and neutral or active, passive and equilibrium. Their various combinations define a set of specific circumstances.

The six-lined hexagram is composed of an upper and lower trigram, giving rise to sixty-four possible combinations. These represent basic archetypal situations. Moreover, each of the six lines describes a degree of change within that situation, reading from the bottom upwards or from the personal to an overall view. The usual method is to throw three coins six times, with the combination of heads and tails producing Yang or Yin lines. The synchronicity of the question and the answer can be significant. The theory is that the universe will respond to genuine enquiries.

The I Ching is a key that can unlock the door to the unconscious. Its language may be obscure, and certainly more subtle than simple yes or no, but it can give unexpected insights into a situation. The I Ching is concerned with both worldly circumstances and moral issues of correct behaviour. The advice is often not to act until the time is right. Many contemplative people regard it as a trusted companion with whom to have confidential conversations. Some kabbalists even call it the "Rabbi I Ching".

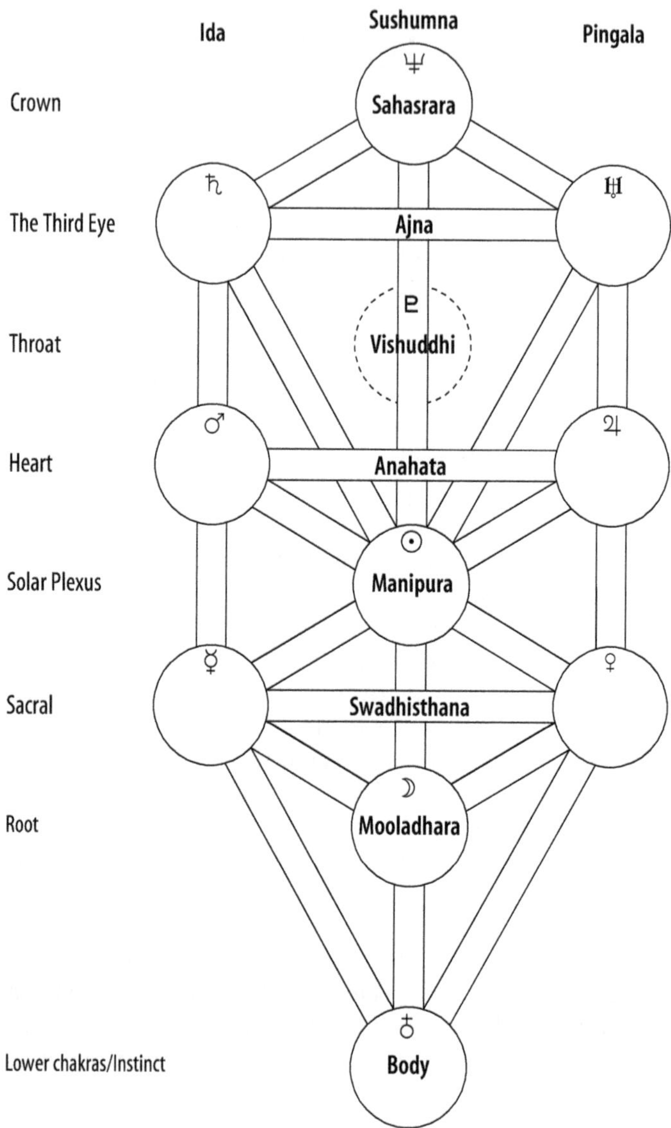

Figure 72—CHAKRAS

The chakras are usually depicted as lotus flowers on the central axis of the human body, indicating seven major energy centres. They are the intermediaries between the electromagnetic field of the physical body and the purely Yeziratic levels of the psyche. The chakras resonate with planetary influences and are part of a cosmic process of potential and development unfolding in time. (Halevi)

68. Levels

The chakra system can be related to kabbalistic astrology on the sefirotic Tree as the seven levels of consciousness and different levels of being. In this context, "being" is the sum total of physical and psychological vitality as well as spiritual refinement.

Like many systems in the physical body, the chakras and the *nadis* that connect them form their own circulation in the subtle vehicle. The chakras are like wheels which keep the energy moving, each vibrating at its own frequency. As every individual is wired differently according to their birth chart, so the chakra experiences vary. Most people are unaware of such subtle processes but the more sensitive individuals do actually perceive a chakra when it is active.

The ancient Indian discipline of yoga aims at activating the chakras by various exercises and techniques. Such spiritual and interior work has an accumulative effect causing the chakras to open naturally at the right moment. Such timing is often synchronised with planetary transits. For example, Uranus can electrify the subtle body while Neptune will make it very sensitive.

One's psychological state of being can also affect the chakras. For example, nervousness can manifest at the sacral level while the heart can be afflicted by anger. If these problems are persistent, they can produce illness in a related part of the body. Conversely, a positive and balanced outlook improves both subtle and physical functions.

On Jacob's Ladder, the Crown chakra is located at the point where the three upper Worlds meet at the Keter of Yezirah. According to tradition, there are also higher chakras above the Crown. These are purely spiritual levels like the Heavenly Halls in Kabbalah.

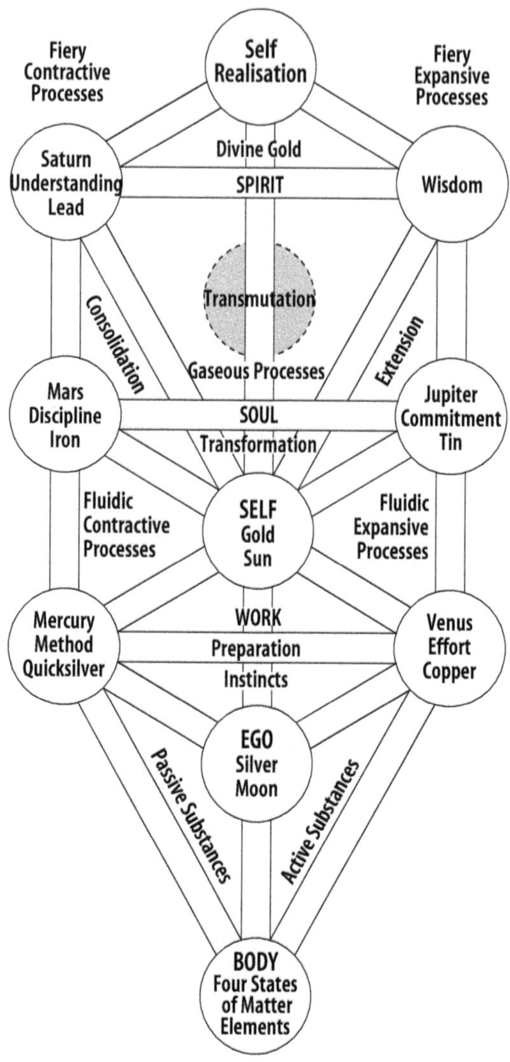

Figure 73—ALCHEMY

The seven known metals were associated with the qualities of the celestial bodies since antiquity. As the Sun illuminates the day and the Moon lights up the night, so their respective metals gold and silver became important symbols in alchemy. The art of metalwork refining these substances from crude ores became, for alchemists, an allegory for interior work. (Halevi)

69. Transformation

Alchemy was practised in medieval Europe as a non-religious form of interior work. The Chinese, Indians, Egyptians, Greeks and Arabs had their own versions of the alchemical discipline. The aim was to produce the Elixir of Life. Unfortunately, many took it literally and sought just physical immortality, not realising it was a system for raising one's level of being and consciousness.

Much was written down in an obscure form. The most striking legacy of alchemy was its imagery. One theme was a retort depicting transmutation in a series of images. For example, the conjunction and separation were repeated seven times indicating a long process through seven levels of sublimation. The skilful use of fire was crucial in alchemical symbolism. Too little would produce no transformation and too much would cause a burnout. A hen hatching her eggs is an often used example of a gentle alchemical fire.

Timing was considered important. An alchemist had to be familiar with astrology as the movement of the celestial bodies through the zodiac generated favourable or unfavourable conditions. Even terrestrial circumstances were taken into account as part of interacting with the universe.

The alchemical Work is a return journey through growth, integration and transformation to the One from which everything originates. The Elixir of Life is a metaphor for the Divine radiance experienced when reaching the level of Azilut. Such deep and refined interior work does indeed have an effect on the biochemistry of the body. The laws of Nature do not allow anybody to live indefinitely but the quality of life will improve. The saying "Those whom the gods love die young" refers to the rejuvenating effect of the Work.

Figure 74—TRACING BOARD
Tracing Boards are contemplative teaching devices setting out various Masonic degrees of initiation or levels of development. This is a Second Degree Tracing Board where the aspirant looks back at the mundane world before starting the ascent towards the Holy Temple. The winding staircase represents Jacob's Ladder. The First Degree Board sets out a general macrocosmic view while the Third Degree depicts a coffin symbolising the potential of transcendental interior life. (19th century print)

70. Freemasonry

The structure of Freemasonry is based on the medieval guilds of stone masons who built the Gothic cathedrals. Contemporary Freemasonry, called speculative in contrast to the medieval operative masons, uses the stone masons' tools as symbols for interior development. Although their overall theme of building Solomon's Temple is biblical, the Masonic view of God is non-sectarian. This made it open to people of any religion.

An Entered Apprentice is required to work on a Rough Ashlar in order to polish the stone into a suitable building block for a Temple. This First Degree is concerned with one's conduct in the physical World. The Second Degree of Fellowcraft is about the soul and morality symbolised by the working tools of testing. The tools of the Master Mason at the Third Degree are used for design and related to creative work at the spiritual level. God is said to be the Master Architect whereas humanity is the Temple.

It is said that speculative Freemasonry began as informal meetings in private homes or taverns in the 17th century. The first Lodges were largely contemplative. Later, with the acquisition of permanent buildings, Grand Lodges were formed and rituals became a prominent feature of Masonic activity. Freemasons were expected to balance off their esoteric interests with charitable work in society. They were a discreet influence in many social reforms. For example, the American Constitution was designed on Masonic principles.

People are attracted to Freemasonry for various reasons, from social contacts to the mysteries of the spiritual path. There is a story about the medieval cathedral builders being asked about their motivation. The first one said, "I have to make a living". The second declared, "I want to become a Master Mason and be respected". The third one said quietly, "I am building for the Glory of God".

Schools Of The Soul

Figure 75—ACADEMY ON HIGH
This painting by John Martin gives an impression of the celestial university of Higher Learning. Those who are capable of operating at the transpersonal level may spend some of their afterlife in such a place. Here is the cutting edge of human development in religion, art and science as well as records of history and past achievements. (John Martin, 19th century)

71. Supervision

The Malkhut of Beriah on Jacob's Ladder is the spiritual component of the Self where the Holy Path begins. The hallmark is goodness and integrity as well as perceiving universal principles. Those who reside in this zone in their afterlife have earned their place by hard interior work while incarnate. Some become the invisible supervisors of others on the Path and the schools of the soul on earth. New ideas may come in dreams or inspiration from this level, often with intellectual objectivity and symbolic creativity.

The Heavenly Halls are inhabited by saints and sages of every genuine tradition. Moreover, a scientist who works with abstracts and higher intellect can be in touch with the World of Ideas. An artist or musician may struggle to express their interior vision but if they succeed they can help other people to shift levels and perceive life in a new way.

Schools of the soul have an important role in the development of humanity. In the ranks of the celestial supervisors there are masters who oversee the continuity of established schools as well as planting seeds for new ones, according to the need of a particular epoch in history. Others may be specialists instructing soul groups or helping individuals in their creative work.

Some people are dimly aware of the presence of their supervisor while others may actually know the identity of their inner teacher. For example, Socrates had his 'Voice' advising him while the eminent Safed kabbalist Joseph Karo had his 'Maggid'. Even ordinary people who are not yet on the Path have their 'guardian angels' or ancestors who guide and protect them if they are worthy.

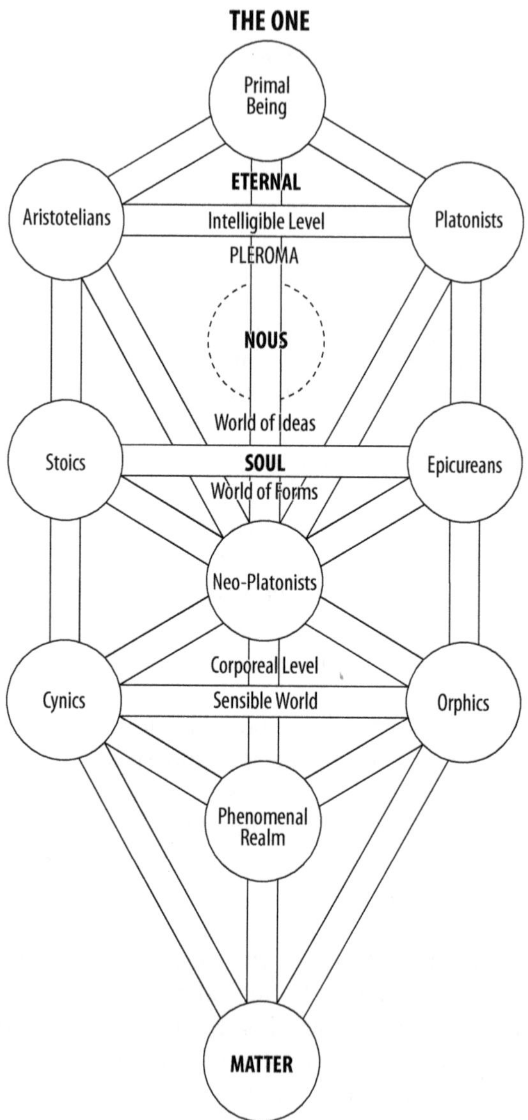

Figure 76—GREEK SCHOOLS

As the Greeks had established colonies along the trade routes around the Mediterranean, many Greeks travelled widely in order to absorb ideas from Middle Eastern cultures. They then developed a metaphysical approach to counterbalance their own and Oriental mythology. Out of this arose the Hellenic schools of the soul and the beginning of Western philosophy. (Halevi)

72. Methodology

While the Greek city-states were frequently at war about who was the most dominant, their intelligentsia were developing a new kind of methodology. In this they sought to define the nature of Matter, the order of the universe and the inner nature of human beings. They relied on observation rather than belief or tradition. Here began the basis of a purely scientific method.

Meanwhile, the philosophical approach was developed. In this individuals looked for an order behind the microcosm of Man and the celestial realm. The study of philosophy was not only about theory but also concerned with improving life according to ethical principles. The school of Pythagoras was a prime example in which the study of mathematics and psychology were part of the curriculum.

Although Socrates was a mystic by inclination, his method was to question everything taken for granted. Two of his students, Plato and Aristotle, applied his approach to philosophy and science which became the side pillars of the Hellenic Tree of knowledge. Later, in Alexandria Plotinus founded the Neoplatonic school that added the middle pillar. This became an important factor of Jewish, Christian and Muslim theology in the Middle Ages.

The Greek approach was already evident in their ancient myths. The stories of the gods and heroes, for example, were so archetypal that modern astrologers and psychologists are still referring to their symbolism when describing phenomena that cannot be defined in purely rational terms. The study of the irrational is also necessary for understanding the complexities of the soul.

Figure 77—TOLEDO

The medieval university city of Toledo in Spain became the Occidental pole to Baghdad, its equivalent in the East. Here the Jewish, Christian and Muslim intelligentsia sought to incorporate Hellenic metaphysics into their traditions. Out of this arose the esoteric lines of Kabbalah, Christian mysticism and Sufi schools of the soul that did not just depend on traditional belief. (19th century print)

73. Dissemination

During the Roman times, the Silk Road brought the Occident and the Orient into contact. Not only goods but books and ideas travelled along the trade routes. Baghdad, a midpoint meeting place, became a centre of learning where enlightened Muslim rulers commissioned the translation of classical Greek manuscripts into Arabic. The scholars were fascinated and inspired by these discoveries.

Many of the manuscripts were brought further west by Jewish merchants who had communities across the Middle East, North Africa and Europe. Toledo in Spain had a school of translators. Their books became available in Spanish, Hebrew and Latin and were in great demand. There was a whole industry of scribes copying books for customers who could afford them.

With the advent of the printing press, a quantum leap in the dissemination of knowledge occurred. More people had access to books and some individuals could even afford to have their own copy. Contemplative study groups were not uncommon. The power of books was enormous as the reader could have an inner dialogue with the text that could be life-changing.

While the oral line can be broken or a unique manuscript can be lost in a disaster, it is not so easy to destroy a book that has been printed in a large number of copies. Even so, both spiritual and secular authorities have burnt books that were considered heretical or dangerous in times of intolerance and oppression.

The Golden Age in Spain came to an end with the Inquisition and the Expulsion of Jews in 1492. When they left, the Jews took their precious books with them.

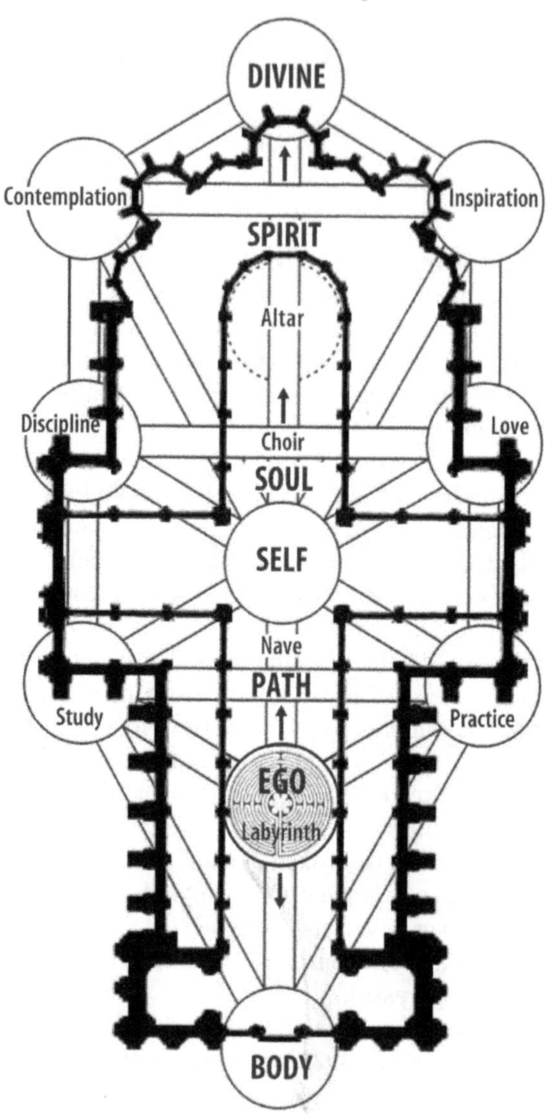

Figure 78—CHARTRES

The architects of Chartres cathedral obviously knew how to design a sacred building. While the elevated ceiling, acoustics and light are awe-inspiring, what is unnoticed is the sefirotic Tree of the ground plan. For example, one has to pass through the circular labyrinth of ordinary mind before approaching the place of the Self at the centre of the transepts. The refined singing of the choir awakens the soul and uplifts it to the sublime level of the spirit at the altar and the Divine beyond. (Prof. Keith Critchlow)

74. Sacred Space

A sacred space represents the interior and higher Worlds amidst ordinary life. Throughout the ages human beings have endeavoured to erect special structures like Neolithic stone circles, pyramids and temples which were a huge communal effort. When used for a long time for religious services, the fabric of the building retains an atmosphere of an uplifting presence.

In most cultures it is also the custom to have a sacred space in private homes. It could be a chapel or just an altar in the corner of a room with symbolic objects and maybe vessels for offerings and rituals. Some people would seek a sacred space outdoors like a rock by a stream or in a forest where they can retreat from everyday life and find peace. Grace can descend anywhere.

Some schools of the soul have acquired buildings that are used exclusively for their sacred activities. Their emphasis may be the Way of Action, Devotion or Contemplation or a combination of these approaches. Such a permanent meeting place can become like a spiritual home for many students.

In the esoteric work it is not unusual to create a temporary sacred space. An ordinary domestic or public setting can be transformed by invoking the Holy Presence for the duration of a group meeting. That also separates a sacred time from secular time. People who travel may take an object or an image to remind them of their own tradition when they are away from home.

The exiled Israelites were weeping by the waters of Babylon for the loss of their Temple. There began the practice of interior ascent called Chariot Riding which was not dependent on a particular place. The Divine connection resides in the inner temple of the soul and the spirit.

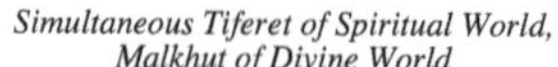

Simultaneous Tiferet of Spiritual World,
Malkhut of Divine World

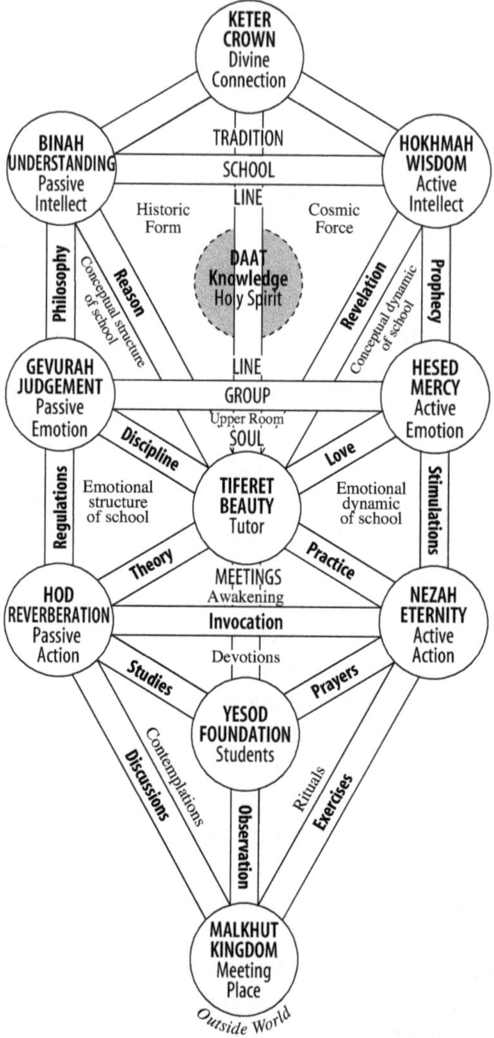

Figure 79—TRAINING

When one enters a school of the soul as a student, an inner alchemy begins to take place. New ideas will challenge one's attitudes and conditioning and often create conflict with old friends outside the school. When the initial enthusiasm called "the Honeymoon" fades, one's commitment will be tested. If one stays, one's whole life becomes more focused. One learns not only from the tutor but from one's companions who may become closer than one's biological family. (Halevi)

75. School of the Soul

It is said that one in a hundred is interested in interior development. One in a hundred of those people actually does something about it like going to public lectures and workshops. Only one in a hundred of those will stay and become committed to the Work. It is not difficult to drift off the Path which is sometimes called "the Razor's Edge" and fall into the habits of vegetable and animal conditioning.

This is why the curriculum of a school of the soul needs to be revised from time to time to meet the need of a particular place and epoch. Yet the basic teaching is universal, for example cosmology and human development as well as ethical values and conduct. The accumulated effort of many schools has lifted human societies from a purely tribal way of life to the level of civilisation. Throughout the ages, schools have flourished particularly in the tolerant cosmopolitan atmosphere of big cities.

However, sometimes animal level political power struggles create such intolerance and hostility that schools have to go underground. The Soviet era of eastern Europe is still within living memory. Any esoteric work was strictly forbidden but people met discreetly, often under disguise. For example, one group practising yoga said they were a physical fitness club when questioned by the secret police. Esoteric books were smuggled in from the West, translated and circulated as typewritten copies amongst trusted companions.

The lifetime of a school can vary from a few decades to several hundred years. It is not unusual that differences of opinions have split schools into two or more independent branches. Schools may come and go but they leave traces of their existence and teaching behind in books and oral tradition. That material can be useful for another school later on.

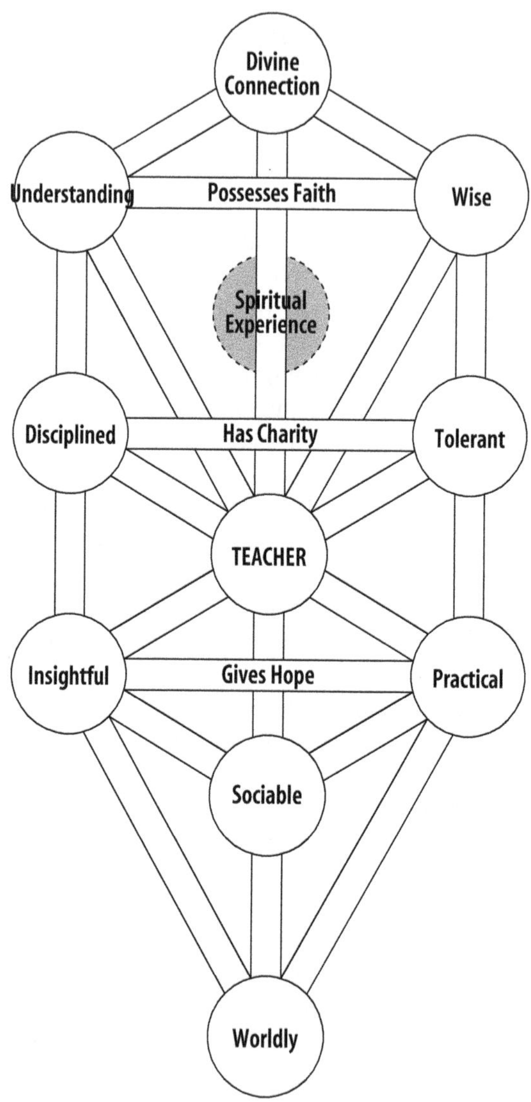

Figure 80—QUALITIES
Some of the characteristics of esoteric teachers are that they are relatively mature and balanced. Scholarly knowledge is not enough. A teacher needs to have a real spiritual connection in order to inspire students as well as enough worldly experience to advise them. Moreover, integrity is vital when dealing with the temptations of power. (Halevi)

76. Teachers

The esoteric proverb “when the student is ready, the teacher will appear” has many implications. The student has to be at a particular turning point to realise that ordinary life is not enough. The Hebrew word ‘kabbalah’ means ‘to receive’. One needs to be receptive and willing to listen. A know-all would not learn much from most teachers.

As in any form of education, there can be several instructors in the course of one’s training. An early teacher may not even be part of a formal school but a wise and experienced individual. It could also be a book that points to a particular direction and to the next step. There are not many masters available and one is fortunate to find a teacher who is at least one week ahead.

There is also a hierarchy of discarnate teachers. In the early stages, one has an inner teacher who is concerned with one’s personal development. Such a teacher is usually in charge of a group of souls. Later, when the student has reached a certain level and is useful to the Work, a specialist teacher of a higher rank will be allocated. Inner teachers are very discreet and do not interfere with the student’s free will. They may indicate what needs to be done but it is the student who has to make the effort and do the work.

The teachers themselves are still in the process of learning yet more. It is said that the best way to learn is to teach. The art of making a tradition interesting can be achieved with increasing experience. Moreover, a teacher in the Tiferet position is sensitive to the students and can lift their level of understanding and insight. A traditional teaching method is to use humour, stories and anecdotes to illustrate universal principles.

Figure 81—CINDERELLA

Cinderella represents the incarnate soul that is confined to the kitchen of the body. This is dominated by the wicked stepmother and two ugly sisters, or the ego and instincts. However her inner teacher, the Fairy Godmother, helps her to shift levels and so meet her soul mate the Prince. Once the soul has woken up and Cinderella has become Self-conscious, the ugly sisters can no longer hide her existence. (Gustave Doré, 19th century)

77. Fables

Fairy tales, fables and parables have been used as teaching methods throughout the ages. They are often moral stories about consequences, cause and effect as well as good and evil. Some also have an esoteric dimension in defining the four Worlds or levels and describing the soul's awakening, trials and transformation. There is often the symbol of a hidden treasure, a Prince or a Princess or some other extraordinary reward at the end.

The story of Cinderella originated in ancient China. Such was its universal appeal that it travelled along the Silk Road and became part of the Western heritage. Cinderella's humble situation was known to her Fairy Godmother who came to help at a crucial moment. Supernatural intervention is often a turning point in an esoteric story.

In another story, a retiring King promised his kingdom to whoever arrived first at his palace. Everybody set off but most stopped at the palace garden where delicious food and drink were served. Those who moved on to the second garden were seduced by beautiful clothes that were freely available. Only a handful arrived at the third garden where they were diverted by magical entertainments. Only one man walked on without being distracted to the palace gates and acquired the Crown. In the story of Aladdin, he had to pass through chambers of copper, silver and gold in order to reach the Lamp in the fourth chamber of the Divine.

The story of Jack and the Beanstalk is clearly a warning about taking psychedelic drugs. The plant takes him up into the higher Worlds where he encounters giants. As he can not handle such powerful cosmic forces, he cuts his connection and the possibility of genuine progress. The esoteric Path is not without temptations and dangers. Inner discipline is vital.

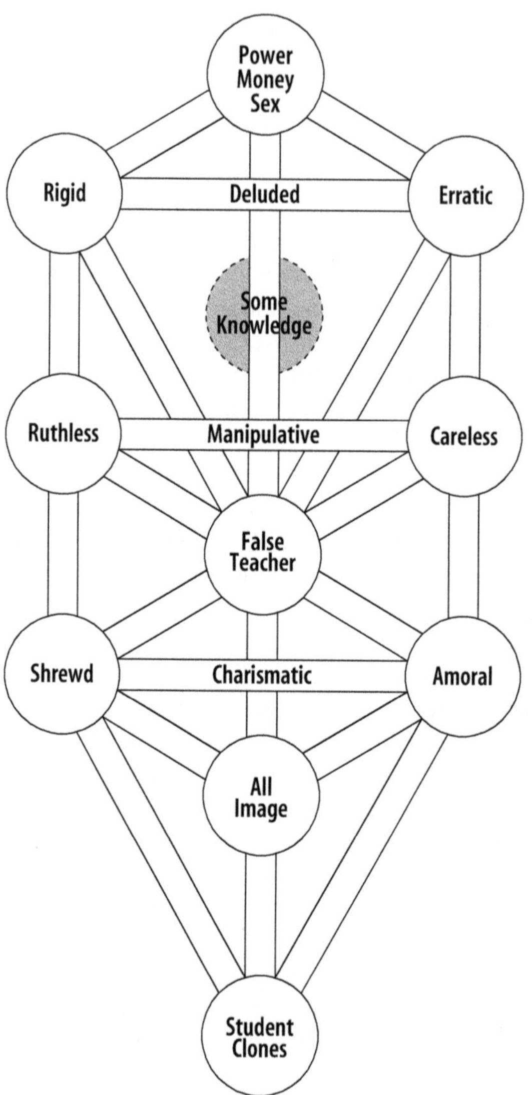

Figure 82—SHADOW

Some teachers and schools set off with good intentions but turn into the opposite if integrity is missing. It can happen especially after the original founder has passed away and animal level people interested in glamour or power take charge of the organisation. Many students have experienced a deep spiritual crisis when they discover that there is something wrong. (Halevi)

78. *Temptations*

The Lucific temptations of money, sex and power can be blatantly obvious or take much more subtle forms. Instead of helping the students to grow, a group or organisation may imprison them in a rigid belief system that does not allow any questioning or independent thought. Some corrupt schools may use spiritual blackmail stating that the outside world should be shunned.

The misuse of power usually begins by making the students become submissive to the teacher and the school's discipline. They are told that in their present state they are inadequate without a map of the Path and no experienced guide. However, the teacher and the school are offering them the right Way. This could take the form of a very tight discipline, reinforced by a uniform mode of dress and manners. A genuine esoteric tradition would not try to control the student's ego or take away their personal freedom. Indeed, the aim is the exact opposite.

A Tiferet temptation that can afflict both the teacher and the students is spiritual pride. Some may be convinced that they alone know the Truth. Such exclusivity creates a view that they are very special or chosen for some spiritual mission. There is much scope for delusions, particularly if there is no coherent teaching or metaphysical system.

The greatest temptation is for the teacher to believe that they are actually the Messiah. It has happened several times throughout history. If there are enough gullible people to support such a claim, a spiritual movement may become just a personality cult. According to esoteric tradition, there is always someone on earth who is indeed the Messiah. However, he or she is usually very discreet and does not need to be known.

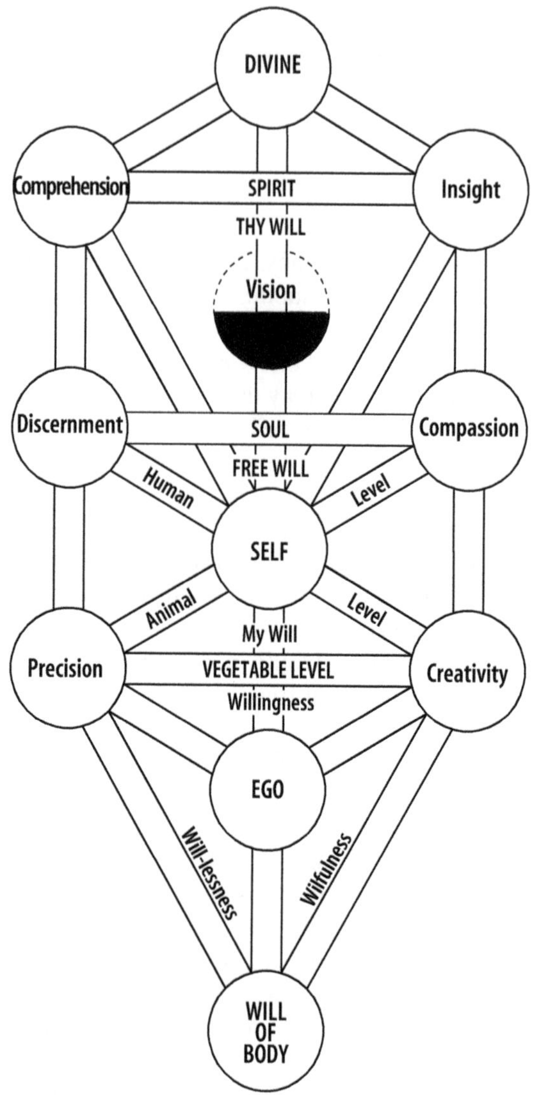

Figure 83—WILLPOWER

Will is consciousness in action. Although one can sometimes have a spontaneous moment of clarity, such an insight may not have any permanent effect. It needs disciplined willpower to maintain such an experience for a period of time. In the early stages of training, one needs to turn inward at will and then expand or deepen one's vision. This takes much practice and the application of esoteric knowledge. (Halevi)

79. Will

The ego at the centre of the three lower triads of action, thinking and feeling is often caught between their different wills. However, the wilfulness of the action triad can be tamed and disciplined. The will-lessness of the thinking processes may be countered by stimulating a particular interest. A characteristic of the feeling triad, the willingness to please others, can be turned into a devotional mode which is vital at the beginning of interior development.

In order to control the lower triads, one needs to rise above one's conditioning. Exercising 'my will' consciously is the beginning of individuation. When one is centred in the Self at Tiferet, then the arrow of attention can be pointed towards a chosen direction.

Human beings have the privilege of free will but only a few exercise it or understand what it means. It is not about wishful thinking but perceiving reality, that is, recognising the pattern of one's fate. Here, at the soul level, one can make life-changing decisions based upon one's real capabilities. Any serious commitment requires free will.

At the spiritual level, one's personal will can be under the guidance of 'Thy Will'. Such a transpersonal view is of quite a different order. Then one is in service to God and accepts one's particular role in Existence, often related to one's destiny.

The central pillar of Jacob's Ladder has access to the four Worlds. It is in essence pure consciousness that has the capacity to gaze into the Mirror of Existence and aid God to behold God through our experience.

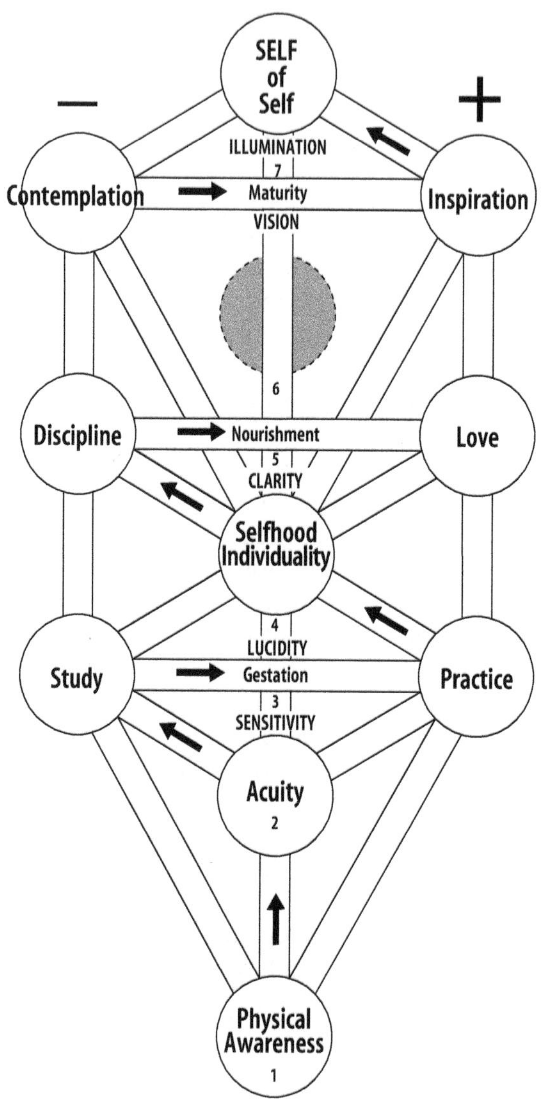

Figure 84—CONSCIOUSNESS
Many esoteric traditions speak of seven levels of consciousness or perception. This progression can be seen on the vertical axis of the psychological Tree. Most stages exist only as potential in the unconscious but can become actual experiences as a result of much interior work. (Halevi)

80. Aim

Besides teaching the general outlines of a tradition, one of the purposes of a school of the soul is to help students to develop and raise their normal level of consciousness. Much theory and practice is designed for this aim. The concentrated effort of a study group creates a supportive and uplifting environment for the individual experience. However, most interior work is done in private.

The student also needs to have a personal aim. At the beginning, it is often nothing less than achieving full enlightenment. To be realistic, one needs to have a short term, a medium term and a long term aim. The will needs to be focused and directed towards a target in order to progress. The aims may change in the course of one's development when new horizons open up.

Increased awareness is the real reward of the Work. For example, the lucidity of the awakening triad can be the beginning of interior freedom. Some call it detachment. The clarity of the soul can discern subtle qualities and significances that are not obvious at the ego level. Those who contemplate transpersonal themes may be granted a cosmic vision or an experience of Divine Grace that illuminates one's whole being.

After such elevated moments, ordinary life may seem dull. Some people despair when they cannot repeat the experience. However, it is normal to have times when the interior riches seem to dry up and nothing appears to be happening. That is often when some deep process of change is taking place in the unconscious. If one perseveres, something new will emerge later. A conversation with one's teacher or companions may offer insights as well as encouragement to continue the Work.

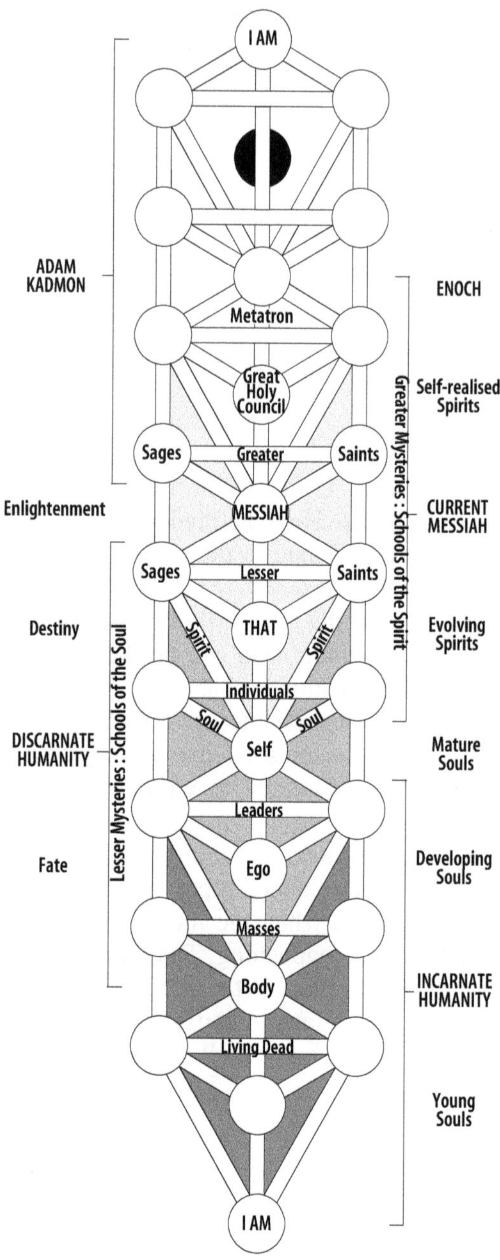
I AM
ADAM
KADMON
ENOCH
Metatron
Great
Holy
Council
Self-realised
Spirits
Sages
Greater
Saints
Greater Mysteries : Schools of the Spirit
Enlightenment
MESSIAH
CURRENT
MESSIAH
Sages
Lesser
Saints
Destiny
Spirit
THAT
Spirit
Evolving
Spirits
Lesser Mysteries : Schools of the Soul
Individuals
Soul
Soul
DISCARNATE
HUMANITY
Self
Mature
Souls
Leaders
Fate
Ego
Developing
Souls
Masses
Body
INCARNATE
HUMANITY
Living Dead
Young
Souls
I AM

81. Progression

In the course of reincarnation, people have to learn certain lessons. In the early stages, they learn from their family the rules regarding what is acceptable or not. In every society, correct behaviour is expected. Thus people have to develop some kind of discipline in order to survive and make progress in the physical World.

Schools of the soul can accelerate personal development as students are taught about the principles that govern human life. With such knowledge comes the responsibility of stabilising one's interior and exterior life as each individual has an effect on the collective level of humanity. Many schools blend in the transpersonal teaching of the spirit which views one lifetime in the context of reincarnation, long term evolution and history.

There are now an increasingly large number of young souls incarnate on Earth. They are guided by more mature souls who have participated in the Work in many lives and in different schools of the soul. Esoteric teachings form a global network of schools which uphold the Light and guide humanity in its progression through all the levels of Jacob's Ladder.

Figure 85 (Left)—DEVELOPMENT

The Divine Name I AM THAT I AM reflects the totality of Existence from the beginning to the end of Time, expressed in the word THAT. Humanity is an important part of that process with its potential for conscious development and Self-realisation. Most of humanity is still immature while old souls are increasingly aware of a vast cosmic drama, overseen by the Holy One who is always present in the Eternal Now. (Halevi)

Figure 86—UNIFICATION

Here a Kabbalist relates to all the four Worlds, both within himself and in the macrocosm. His physical body is the result of organic evolution while his soul resonates with the Solar system. His spirit reflects the World of Creation while having his Divine origin in Adam Kadmon. To contemplate all these elements is part of the Work of Unification. (Halevi)

82. The Work

The esoteric proverb 'know thyself' is a personal working method. It requires observing the mineral, vegetable and animal levels as well as developing human individuality. The higher levels of the psyche and the spirit are inevitably involved in maintaining the Divine connection.

Kabbalah is a contemplative discipline as well as a mode of meditation and action. It is a way to increase one's understanding of Existence. Learning the theory is necessary but applying the principles of the Tree of Life and Jacob's Ladder in all aspects of life is also very important as real knowledge comes from actual experience.

Sometimes the Work is said to have three distinct stages. At the beginning one works for oneself, then also for fellow companions. Later one works for the school or the tradition. A living Teaching is the result of a long chain of transmission and the contribution of committed individuals throughout history.

While one can achieve much, the Work continues. An ancient kabbalistic method is "keep practising!".

Lightning Source UK Ltd.
Milton Keynes UK
UKHW021157220921
391011UK00009B/236